Bill Patton
Your Address

Your phone number
Your e-mail address

(Your agent's name)
(Your agent's address)

3

TOP 5 STRATEGIES AND TACTICS FOR WINNING TENNIS

by Bill Patton

Early Reviews

I really enjoyed reading Top 5 Strategies and Tactics..., It's amazing how many match situations Bill is able to cover and is able to give solutions and goals for just about any level of player. This book is a must read for any competitive player out there looking to reach the next level!
Michael Joyce, WTA Tour Coach
(Formerly Coach of Maria Sharapova for 6 years)

This is a remarkable book when it comes to Strategies and Tactics for tennis. It is very refreshing and clear the pathway used by the author to introduce the two concepts and explain how to utilize them when playing tennis. He presents very practical situations (real stories) related to the topics that immediately help the reader better understand how to benefit from this gained knowledge and implement it into their game. I strongly recommend this book it will help players of all levels."
Julio Godreau
Director of Tennis, Mississippi Tennis Academy
Jackson, Mississippi

This book serves as a great fundamental overview of strategies and tactics in tennis. A wealth of useful and actionable information can serve as the knowledge base from which a player and/or coach makes decisions or starts the conversation. Bill is very thoughtful in his caring ways of making sure the player understands long term implications related to choices made. This is the kind of book I would like all my students to read.
Alexander Johansson
Director of Shark Tennis Academy at Corpus Christi Country Club
Founder of Hoplu App

Bill has written a very good, executable series on Strategy and the tactics to use. I'm impressed with his knowledge and the way he imparts it to readers so they can easily understand. I also enjoyed the real life matchplay experiences included.
Riaz Shivji
Founder / Owner
RS Tennis Academy
San Mateo, CA

The Top 5 Tennis Strategies illustrates an accurate and simplified version of teaching tennis. I find it very helpful and right on the target. Certainly a tennis book worth buying. When published I will recommend it to all of our coaches in Israel.
Aviram Markovich
High-performance Tennis Coach and Club Manager
Tennis Krayot
Haifa, Israel

As a new tennis coach whose experience focused on the volleyball courts more than the tennis courts, Tennis Strategies and Tactics led me in the right direction with insight on basic strategy. I know I will be a better coach to my players by utilizing and reinforcing tactics outlined in this ebook.
Darlene Hoke
Head Tennis Coach
Lake Minneola High School
Lake Minneola, FL

For everyone who wants to play smart Tennis, to win matches with a game plan.

Do you want to gain even more value from this book?

Join my book group by sending an email to 720DegreeCoaching@gmail.com and putting "Join Book Group" in the subject line.

You will receive an invitation to my email list. When you accept that, I will then send some additional materials. When you buy this print book, you get both eBooks Free with purchase. Top 5 Strategies and Tactics and Top 5 Mental and Emotional Foundations will be yours in eBook form.

I will then send out some information on upcoming projects, events, books, and other educational opportunities for you, my ideal reader.

You will also have the opportunity to get books when they go on sale for ridiculously low prices.

Books by Bill Patton

The Art of Coaching High School Tennis

Playing Sports Right: Your Way

Be Present for the Precious Moments in Tennis: A Conversation with Torben Ulrich (eBook)

My Awesome Tennis Journal

Match Play and the Spin of the Ball in the 21st Century (eBook)

How to End Cheating in Junior Tennis: 21 Ways to Eat an Elephant

Tennis Coaches and Parents: Bridging the Communication Gap

Who am I to help you win more matches? I am a guy who is passionate about teaching and coach tennis. I am a 27 year tennis veteran of the Tennis Industry mainly as an USPTA Elite and PTR Tennis Professional. I have a B.S. in Industrial Psychology and have written a Master's Thesis in Education. These pieces help to prepare me for this experience – being able to share my perspective with other coaches is an honor. Through my experience and education, I hope to give you a better perspective in regard to planning and playing strategy.

I consider myself a lifelong learner. I have enthusiastically read over 100 books about tennis new and old, popped at least 50 VHS and DVDs into the machine, and attended over 40 Professional Tennis Conferences. I have developed a reputation as someone who might ask the tough question. I have also learned quite a bit from my blog radio show; which you can listen to at Blog Talk Radio - 720 Degree Coaching. When you join my email list, you gain access to the full catalog of radio shows. They can also be downloaded as an MP3. All of this is done to help for your improvement! Join the email list here.

I take great pride in the fact that when I get involved in a program, my players are the ones who improve as fast or faster than any other players in my area. My goal here is to help you improve significantly. There is so much information available, I couldn't convey it all directly to my other students. You have a big advantage. In fact, I invite you to become my student today. Of course, you should have a coach with whom you work closely. Use these readings to help you come up with some great questions that will help increase the value of your lessons. In the case that you and I agree, and your coach does not, it's worth exploring why not. You may then you may want to shop for a coach who is a better fit for you. Please share this book with your coach, they may want to read it with great interest.

If you are a high school coach looking for resources, you may also enjoy The Art of Coaching High School Tennis. Also, if you reading the eBook version of this title be sure to look for the next book in this series coming in a matter of weeks.

It has been quite satisfying to have worked with students at all levels. Some students started with me, some I worked with early in their development. Others have moved on to attain a higher level and became Division 1 college players or professional players. However, the fact that even more of my former players became Tennis coaches, says much more about how well we collaborated during that time.

Ultimately, it's the value that you receive from reading this book and others that matters much more than any perceived credentials I may have. I am sharing the most helpful information I can find to serve you the best way possible to help grow the sport of Tennis. Thank you for reading.

Thank you to Dede Allen for her great help in editing this edition. She selflessly contributed her feedback on style and content. All the reviewers who took time read it and either posted on a book review outlet, or contributed a review in the early part of this book. Shaun Frazeur tirelessly made revisions to the cover art. Alexander Johansson also gave of his time and effort in various ways. The Real Tennis Coaches Professional Dialogue on Facebook for allowing me to post pieces of this for their approval even in rough draft form, too many people to mention made great comments, thank you to all of you!

Bill Patton 7/30/2015

The Fundamentals of Strategy and Tactics

To fully understand strategy, we also need to understand how tactics fit or do not fit with the strategy you may have chosen. Note the Venn Diagram (you may want to explain that to the readers – or show a picture) and inside of the larger circle Strategy are three smaller circles tactic 1, tactic 2 and tactic 3. Also note that tactic 4 is outside the circle.

To add some flesh and bones to what is written here I will tell a short story to illustrate the point of strategy and tactics:

Tactics that Fit a Strategy

Shreyas had a tough match looming, He had recently become a full time serve and volley player; he had not yet fully gained confidence in his ability to beat a top player using this new strategy exclusively. He was worried about an upcoming sectional tournament match, because the opponent had incredible topspin groundstrokes and seemed to really love to hit passing shots more than anything. As is true of some players, the opponent enjoyed having a target at the net to sharpen his focus. So we put our heads together, and came up with the 'kitchen sink' strategy of working very hard to disrupt the rhythm of the opponent. Knowing that players with heavy topspin games feature power and placement require one thing: a relatively consistent ball coming to them so they can time their shot. Shreyas' job on the day would be to completely mix things up and destroy the possibility of his opponent developing any consistency. As a side note, this is one reason why I don't like when players say, "I need to be more consistent", because it can actually play right into the hands of your opponent.

The 'kitchen sink' is my colloquial expression for using a disruptive strategy and it consists of every shot you can think of to hit. Essentially, it means hitting no two shots alike. The strategy was maximum rhythm disruption, and the tactics were to hit the ball: Fast then slow, high then low, more Spin, less Spin, opposite Spin, cross court, down the line, up the middle. The tactic that was NOT in the strategy was to rally consistently or try to out hit the opponent.

Shreyas did very well and winning the first set while surprising his opponent with the strategy. His opponent seemed to blame himself for playing poorly, but we knew that it was the effect of strategy that was beating him. Then Shreyas almost made a fateful ongoing mistake. For three games in the second set he went away from the strategy, using tactics that did not fit the strategy. He began to 'hit' with the opponent, giving him the consistently powerful shots that work well for him, the opponent won those three games very quickly. Those 3 games seemed like they were over in less than 10 minutes and a momentum shift had occurred in the match. The opponent won the second set due to this turnabout. However, Shreyas went back to the original tactics that fit within the strategy of disruption, winning the match convincingly in the third set. One of the most valuable aspects of the high school tennis experience is that a coach can remind the player about the game plan and help get them back on track. This gives the player a better tennis education, one that they can use in future matches.

When selecting a strategy, be sure that the tactics you select are in line with that same strategy. I also encourage you to remain open minded, because you may discover a shot or a sequence that works on that day in that match, so you can include that in your game plan. Be aware changes to your tactics that support or do not support your strategy, then manage them moving forward. Finally if you are down a set and a break, you either need to play much better, or switch to plan B. I have seen quite a few matches where a player has chosen the current game plan, and is down a set and break and either elevates their level of play, or the game plan begins to take a cumulative effect on the opponent and will now be truly effective and lead to the best chance of victory. The rest of this book will breakdown a menu of game plans: A, B, C, D, and E, but you can order them in any way you choose, but they must fit with your current skill set. If your skill set is limiting you, get out and take a lesson. Build your game one lesson at a time.

#

The Basics of Tennis Strategy

As you look at some of the foundations of Tennis strategy, consider your skill set. You can enter this system at any of the five entry points, these are the different game plans A, B, C, D, E. Here is where you will take the list and put it in the order that works for you best. From there it's up to you which of the other four you want to explore and expand on to develop a B, and a C game. Very few people can effectively work all five of the strategies contained herein, but you will win many more matches if you at least have a B game to shift to in time of need. So, let's take a look at some foundational truths of tennis strategy. This eBook was inspired by a parent with whom I was discussing 'A comprehensive book' on strategy. She asked "Will it cover the basics?", to which I said "Of course". At which point I made a mental note to cover the basics. However, just because these things are basic, does not necessarily make them easy. Later, this book will become part of a compilation with all my other works on strategy into one large print book which will be available in 2015.

The hierarchy of how to win points, or not lose them easily

When first learning Tennis take these following concepts in order from most basic to the most advanced:

1. Get the ball in play, even if you have to lob, or bunt the ball back.
2. Choose a direction, down the line, cross court or down the middle.
3. Hit to a direction and to the depth that you choose (deep/short, short/deep shot combinations can be deadly).
4. Choose a spin. This hierarchy differs from Match Play and the Spin of the Ball,whereBill Tilden (Match Play and the Spin of the Ball) states "Every

ball must be hit with some type of intentional spin”
5. Using the Speed of Your Shot or Power Tennis.

The actual training of power and speed and where it fits on the list is subject to great debate. Suffice it to say that if you can overpower your opponent without dramatically increasing your errors, you should do it. The full range of thought on this is varies extremely from: “Hit it as hard as you can, until it starts to go in” and “Play like a man or woman” to “Control and accuracy are what the game is really about, and you would suffer a temporary loss of those while learning incrementally more power, so for now just keep it in”. You can also intentionally change speeds on your shots.Those that say that powerful tennis is the only effective tennis, might say that the ceiling of what can be achieved with power will be diminished if you are preoccupied with control in your developmental stages. The other group would say that you may lose confidence early if you lose a lot of matches by playing a high risk game, while other young players are playing in a very controlled fashion early on in their tennis career. It can be instructive to us, that the players who are very successful in the younger age ranges are not usually very successful in the older age ranges when more power is rewarded more often. Young kids under age 12 lack power, so they can win with a keep it in style, later they will be beaten by players who have mastered one of the other four strategies. The question becomes, what is your strategy for now, and which strategy do you want to develop in your game? As a coach, I expose my players to every strategy available.

Strategy One: Get and Keep the Ball in Play

The most important aspect of Tennis is getting and keeping the ball in play. This does not mean necessarily mean 'be consistent', because being consistent may mean putting the ball in play in a way that your opponent really loves. The phrase 'be consistent' is far too non-specific, and usually leads to unreasonable expectations in regard to how often a player can put the ball in play. I have never heard a player come off the court saying "I was happy with my consistency today". How can we make this instruction more specific, so as to be helpful?

When getting the ball in play, work hard to avoid your opponent's favorite shot, or you will find it very difficult to keep the in play, if you are constantly under attack. Once I had the chance to coach a high ranked junior player while helping a high school coach, because I wanted to be helpful. The high ranked junior who should have been much more intelligent kept saying "I need to be more consistent". My message to her was "You can keep the ball away from the opponent's preferred strike zone", to which she responded "I feel like I need to be more consistent". I tell that story to underscore what has become a not very thoughtful approach to the game with consistency.

You can work very hard to keep the ball to toward the outside edges of the court. Another thing to consider is the question "Who is the better player at making angled shots in this match?" If it's you, then by all means make some angled shots, however if it's your opponent, then you may want to direct more balls deep down the center of the court. Be sure to hit the ball deep when you hit down the middle of the court, because if you drop the ball in the center of the court every time, your opponent will have a great day with those more often than not. It sounds so simple, but there are some subtleties to keeping the ball in play. Especially notice the height and speed of shot that is their favorite and avoid hitting that one. Every shot has some risk associated with it, so if you are expecting to make 100% of your low-risk shots, then you have an unreasonable expectation.

The numbered paragraphs below give you some reasonable

expectations and objectives for your match that will help you at least to not beat yourself. Until you have mastered most of what is below, I do not recommend that you move on to more complex strategies and tactics. Here you will see the rationale for allowing for some errors, because every shot has a risk/reward ratio. The following progression of strategies and tactics move from low risk/low reward to high risk/high reward ratios.

#

Tactics that Support the Strategy

"Get and Keep the Ball in Play"

First Serve Percentage

Your first serve percentage is still the #1 factor in deciding the outcome of your match. No matter what your strategy is, a high first serve percentage is part of that. Since the serve is the single most taxing shot in the game that you regularly hit, you will save quite a bit of mental and emotional energy by developing a reliable first serve. If need be, aim for the very center of the service box and 3 feet inside the service line for the safest possible target.

Players sometimes don't realize that when you make your first serve, you actually serve fewer serves, thus keeping you fresh for a longer period in the match. Additionally, it is nearly universal that players win a higher percentage of points when they make their first serve, than when they make their second serve.

There is also a psychological aspect of getting your first serve in, as opponents generally are less ready to attack your first serve, than they are second serve. Opponents become more confident, hopeful and aggressive when returning second serves.

If you make your first serve, you will never double fault.

However; there is a limiting factor when it comes to high serve percentage. Your first serve could become a non-aggressive shot for the sake of trying to make much more than 70% of your serves in play. If you settle for a slightly lower first serve percentage, you will be able to put a little more on you first – you may enjoy less pressure and be able to hit a more effective serve. Some players are blessed with plenty of power and often have serves that cannot be returned very easily, so a serve percentage around 60% can still very effective. Players lacking power, will want to make their serves in the court around 70% of the time, but it's important for them to do all they can to use some power, vary spins, or go for various placements to keep the opponent off balance. Many players unwittingly place their serve into the opponents' forehand every time, because they have made no thought of doing anything else. However, if you are a fairly new player, simply start by getting the first serve in the box, even at the risk of it going to the opponent's forehand.

To show the difference in how serves can vary in effectiveness, consider the two extremes: the power player, and the player who may lack some power, but has a wide variety of serve spins and placements. There was a well noted player who lacked power on his serve, but was very fast around the court. Over much of his career he served 70% first serves in the court, and won 60% of those points. Let's call that an effectiveness quotient of .42 when you multiply the two together. Another noted player who served 50% of first serves in play won 80% of the points for an effectiveness of .40. You can make an argument that the player with less power was more effective. What he lacked was the ability to hit a big serve and erase a break point at a big moment. It's really a great idea to consult with a coach to find out which player are you, and what do they recommend for you to pursue for your ultimate best game.

When I have a player who is capable of hitting big serves, but they hold back for whatever reason, I make it my first task to help them unleash what may be the be most effective part of their game. One particularly difficult problem is a player who is a afraid to take risks, but has been blessed with incredible power potential. If that is you, I would strongly recommend that you learn to play fearlessly, and again, seek coaching to find ways to play the power game with intelligence, and in an effective way, so that you can keep the ball in play. You should know that if you are blessed with great power, you ought not to obsess about keeping the ball in play, because the best offensive players in tennis also have a high tolerance for making more errors than more conservative players.

#

Return of Serve Percentage

Make your opponent work hard to win their service game. You can create a cumulative effect of stress that increases as the match goes on for them. One key element of making your opponent work hard to hold serve is to return 80% of all serves coming to you. It's much more important to make your opponent play the next ball after the serve than it is to hit an occasional winner. This is when you want to avoid making any unnecessary errors on returns. You don't have to hit the ball back hard, you simply need to get it in play. Some great players are well noted for returning incredibly fast serves, by simply putting their racket out and tapping it back, using the power on the incoming serve as all that is needed to send it back into play.

The safest option for getting the ball back in play is to attempt to strike the ball right back at the server, because hitting it back the same direction makes it much easier to time your shot. Also, when you aim down the middle of the court, you can miss your target by 13.5 feet and it will still be in the court. Once you find you can return serve without a lot of difficulty, then you can steer the majority deep crosscourt, while sometimes going for a bit more angle or surprise the server with an occasional down the line return. Keep your focus on making the returns; if you are going for too much, you are letting the server off the hook with easy point wins. A good guideline is that you can attempt to miss only one return per service game. Once you have missed a second return, it's a great idea to become more conservative, in order to make it tough on the opponent.

As you advance in levels, a more aggressive return game becomes important. The idea here is not to award the server a free point, by missing your return. serve. A good mantra to hold in your mind is "make them play". This means that they should have to hit at least two shots or more to win a point. If you do not return serve well, your only hope of winning is to get lucky stringing a few returns together, and hope for a double fault or two, and maybe winning tiebreakers. The best players in the world are always accomplished serve returners.

Movement to the Return

It has been said that 80% of serves will land within one step of where you are returning. With those 80% coming within one step, strive to hit close to 100% of those back, you won't make them all, but have a mindset that you can. 20% of serves will be two or more steps away, so work to hit at least 50% of those back. That may mean some lunging and stretching to get a racket on the ball at times, but two quick steps and you might find it's not that hard to bunt them back. Note: going through a proper warm up is one of the subtle factors that will help you on your return as you prepare for the wild twists and turns you will need in order to make some of these shots. Future eBooks will cover this topic more thoroughly. If your opponent has a monstrous serve, you must strive to make them play more shots, while conceding that some of those serves are just too tough. Be emotionally flexible and give credit to your opponent for having a strong serve.

Note: While I absolutely forbid doing this in any kind of sanctioned play, I have been known to say in a social match with a friend "Wow, that's a great serve. How do you do that?", knowing fully that if they stop to think about how they do it, then its likely they wont serve as well after that. As a coach and friend, I want to make sure that players experience what that kind of gamesmanship can do to your game, so that you can protect yourself from it in the future. When people have tried that same tactic on me, I answer "I don't know how I do it, but here comes another one!". Players who use gamesmanship are trying to get you off your game, and if they can succeed at that, then they can make it more difficult for you to keep the ball in play.

Finally, be a keen observer of patterns that your opponent uses. Do they have a certain place they serve for the first point? For example, at 30-15 or 15-30, do they have a serve or placement they like? More importantly do they have a serve they use often on break point or game point? When you start to tune into a pattern you can then react better when you recognize the same serve coming. Knowing where they often serve and/or prefer to serve, you can change your positioning to cover those much better. Sometimes you can take a position to try to force them to hit another serve. Some opponents are so well trained to hit their second serve only to the backhand that if you move far enough over that you can hit a forehand. This may render them helpless, and may miss a serve or be less effective when going outside their comfort zone.

The former math teacher in me says "If you make 90% in play out of the 80% that are within one step, and 50% in play out of the 20% that are two more more steps away, that's 72 and 10, and you will have returned 82% of the serves". Make the server play!

#

Deep Shots in a Rally

Once the rally has begun, when you hit the ball directly down the middle, you can miss by 13.5 feet and you will still not hit the ball wide. When you aim deep crosscourt, you also gain 4.5 more feet to hit into as opposed to down the line shots. Hitting down the line gives you 78 feet, but crosscourt the diagonal length of the court is 82.5 Feet. Going for a little height and depth makes gravity your friend by helping to the ball in the court. Trying to rip an impressive, but less effective lower percentage shot just barely over the net can make gravity your enemy - making the ball go into the net. It has been disproven the value of the net being lower in the middle, as the net is further from you on a crosscourt shot than it is on a down the line shot. When you are playing deep shots, It's a far better surprise to have a ball land in, that you thought was going out, than to have it hit the net when you thought it might go over. When you are aiming for deep shots, you will pay more attention to the deep part of the court, then you will avoid the net quite often, because your eyes and mind are not focused on it as an obstacle to overcome, because you have shifted your focus to locations further in the court.

Up to a certain level of play 75% of errors by the average player go into the net. If you focus on hitting the ball a bit higher over the net, it will result in fewer errors. You have no chance of your opponent hitting the shot back if it is in the net, but, you do have a chance of them playing a long ball. Your errors will decrease. When I am training players for the first time to keep their balls deep in the court, and I ask them to hit the ball out long, they discover that its actually harder than it looks.

Hitting your groundstrokes deep crosscourt is the way to build your points. Two books come to mind that you can read to support this notion. Dr. Allen Fox's "Think to Win" and Paul Wardlaw's "Pressure Tennis" have been quite helpful to me personally and my players when it comes to winning more matches. I recommend them highly. You will find some great drills in Wardlaw's book. I see those books as more detailed studies for those that want to be very successful Tennis Players or coaches.

Essentially, you will build your points with crosscourt shots, showing patience, waiting for a short ball or a down the line ball, then you can attack with a down the line shot. The deeper you can safely hit the ball crosscourt, the more likely you are to draw a weak reply that you can attack. What constitutes a weak reply is predicted on your ability to take advantage of opportunities and ability to recognize them.

Know Your Game and Your Future Game

It's wise to have a long term plan for what kind of player you want to be. Your style should be a reflection not only of your growth in character, but match your physique and special abilities. Some people are more powerful and explosive, others are more cautious and have better fine motor control. If you are the explosive player, (yes, of course you do have to keep most balls in play), you have much more to gain from playing a higher risk game than your counterpart who has better fine motor control. Players neurotically use the phrase “Be more consistent”, not realizing what there true application of that phrase really means. What they should be thinking is “never miss”; everyone misses at some point, players shouldn’t obsess over missed shots. Player should instead be working toward playing intelligent Tennis using calculated risk, realizing that really almost any shot can be missed. On the other hand, if you are missing shots often, that can easily be made, then you definitely want to check in with a Tennis Professional to help you with that.

As you gain experience, and are ready to move beyond getting and keeping the ball in play, start developing a plan for building new tactics into your game, at the right time. I have seen quite a few players who were taught to play according to a coach or academy’s philosophy, even though it was a ‘cookie cutter’ approach. Are you a cookie? NO! So learn and train according to your strengths, and learn to mitigate your weaknesses. It’s not likely to happen if you are trying to learn to play like someone who had different strengths.

#

A Different Approach on Second Serve Return

On first serve return you generally want to make the other player play another shot. On second serve you want to be on the attack. However, you don't want to miss more than 1 out of 5 attacking shots.

There is also a fairly large amount of spontaneity that comes with attempting to return serve. When your opponent hits a strong serve that goes right into your ‘wheel house’, then you may be able to crush it, as a high percentage play. Sometimes pathetic second serves can travel so slowly that timing the shot becomes an issue, and it’s possible to botch an attempt to attack. Don’t be discouraged.

How well you make your opponent play, and how well you attack second serves are the second most important factor in a match. If the first serve puts someone ahead in a point, then a great return equalizes it. If a second serve puts the player in a neutral position, then a great return gives the returner the lead in the point.

On the Day of The Match

When you warm up, focus mainly on rhythm and placement. It's pretty simple advice.

Mental Skills: Keeping the Ball in Play

When you are playing a "keep the ball in" strategy, there are two main mental skills you will want to focus on from point to point. The first skill to develop is paying attention to your effort level, maintaining as close to 100% as you can, and notice any dips in effort. Keeping the ball in play is also known as "The High Effort Game", so it's essential to work on that.

Concentration is the other mental skill. Two things that will help your overall concentration are:

1. Allowing your eyes to rest for a few moments between points.
2. Using much of the 90 seconds changeover to rest your concentration.

When you attempt to concentrate in every moment of a match you will certainly become quite fatigued. Resting your mind for moments at a time will prolong your ability to concentrate over a longer period.

Using Depth Control to Pressure Opponent's Movement

The player who has the ability to control the depth of their shot has quite an advantage over the player that cannot control depth. With today's new rackets which feature less dense string patterns, the 'angle of deflection' from a Tennis racket is much higher than it was in the past. This will aid a player tremendously at hitting more spin, having a higher trajectory over the net, and thus more depth. The question for that player is, can they sufficiently adjust the angle of their racket head at contact to also hit shorter and sharper angled shots? This is a great subject for which to consult a Tennis Professional in your area.

Tactics at the top of the list for depth control:

Keep the ball as deep as possible on every shot during a rally, until the opponent hits a shorter ball. Keeping the ball deep during the rally, keeps your opponent pushed further back in the court, making it very difficult for them to hurt you with their shot. Although, there are times when some low percentage shots can be made by the opponent. Don't get discouraged if your opponent can win 10% of the points while pushed way back in the court.

When both players are keeping the ball deep, of course there is some risk of an error long, however, that is an acceptable error to make any time the ball is only out by a foot or two. If you are missing by much more than that its time for a change. You can only learn to control the ball deep in the court, by risking the occasional out ball. If many balls are deep and you are losing, then it's probably time to go back to 'keeping the ball in play'.

The best definition I have seen for a deep shot is one that lands in the second half of the large rectangle. If you have seen a 60' court, the line that exists marking 60' is perfect, so focus on hitting beyond that line. The 60' mark is 9' in from the baseline. If you keep your ball in the last nine feet of the court you will be very tough to beat. This will keep your opponent moving sideways or even backwards to hit the ball. A fairly large percentage of the time, when two players engage in a very deep rally, and one of them is the first to unintentionally hit short, the other player gains a very large advantage in the point. That player can now move forward and will have at least two different options of where to hit the next ball to put their opponent under pressure.

#

Directional Shots Pressure Their Movement

Whenever I coach at match at any level, a constant piece of advice that I give my players is 'Build your points with cross court shots.' Crosscourt play gives you not only more court for which you to hit into by 4.5 feet, but also has the potential of pushing your opponent much further back and to the side of the court than down the line shots. Dr. Allen Fox explained in his book "Think to Win" how the notion of 'Hit it where they aren't' is not a good idea if the down the line shot seems open, just because your opponent is not standing in that spot. When you go for a down the line shot that does not significantly pressure your opponent, that allows your opponent to hit the ball crosscourt and immediately pressure your movement. When you rally crosscourt patiently, you may find a time to hit a slightly more aggressive angle, which can tilt the point in your favor. In the meantime, the amount of moving you will need to recover to an ideal for the potential shots of your opponent will be less.

When it comes to the adage "Control, Hurt, Finish", controlling the point is where the crux of this strategy lies. When you find yourself in a rally, both players are attempting to maintain control of the rally. Crosscourt shots help you to maintain control of the rally. When one player hits the ball short, or goes down the line without hurting the other player, then that player has a prime opportunity to Hurt you with their shot. If you are disciplined in regard to building points with deep crosscourt play, you will find that you can control the points better, and your opponent will more often be the one that gives you a chance to hurt them with an angle or a down the line shot on your terms.

In actual practice you may find that the system of Control, Hurt, Finish may end at any time. In the midst of controlling points, your opponent may miss their shot. While attempting a shot to hurt your opponent, you may 'accidentally' hit a winner

#

Depth Control for Advancing Players

Advanced players may have the ability to hit a lower shorter shot intentionally and with enough directional control, that it puts their opponent off balance. One example of this would be a Roger Federer short slice shot to an opponent with a two handed backhand, keeping the ball low, really forcing that opponent to run forward and bend low to make the shot. When Andre Agassi switched to a strategy primarily based on keeping the ball very deep in the court and his opponent moving around at the back, he experienced very lengthy periods at the top of the ATP game. Rafael Nadal has been quoted as saying when asked about his strategy in a match, “I hit a lot of heavy topspin deep to the backhand, pretty simple, no?” One principle to observe is that when a player combines extreme athleticism with great technique, or even unique technique, they create a match up problem for their opponent that allows them to play a fairly simple strategy.

A deep serve will keep your opponent pushed back as much as possible. Short serves can create easier opportunities for the opponent to gain the offensive in a point immediately.

Shot combinations that feature one deep ball and one shorter ball and vice versa are one of the best staples for a winning game. When you are able to control and vary the depth of your shots the amount of pressure you can put on your opponent improves dramatically. By doing this you introduce a different element - your opponent must move diagonally up or back for the shot. One classic shot combination that I teach to all my players is to hit a topspin shot on a short angle that lands near the service line on one side of the court, followed by a deep shot to the opposite corner, or vice versa. It does not matter whether you have intentionally or accidentally hit the first shot in the sequence, you can follow up with the second shot and you will find you have taken an opportunity to create a great shot combination.

Keeping the ball very low and short can be a great strategy against a heavy topspin player, tall players, or those who hit very flat balls, but you must have extremely effective slice and flat shots to make it work.

On the Day of the Match

Warm up by hitting the ball out long. For a few minutes in your practice at the beginning you and your partner can work to hit the ball 3 to 5 feet out, then shift to hitting toward the baseline and finally a few feet inside. Make sure you get great length on shots in the warm up, as you may have some difficulty in the match if you tighten up at all.

Mental Skill: Pressuring Your Opponent's Movement

Eliminate a fear of hitting long. Learn to very much despise hitting the first short ball in a rally. Have something that you tell yourself if your ball goes long. I like "At least I am being aggressive with my depth" or "OK, now I just need to hit it 3 feet shorter for a shot with great depth" or something along those lines. One great benefit of this depth seeking is that you will lose sight of the net, and very few balls will go into the net because of the shift in your focus.

Also, come to the realization that you might not execute your shot combinations perfectly in a point. That might mean that you have to start over in the point. Also be ready to capitize on accidental shots that become the first shot of a combination, and smartly make the second shot in that combination. Always be alert to opportunities.

Strategy: Pressure your Opponent' s Time and Space

Pressuring your opponent's time and space can be done in different ways. You can start with the serve, and continue in a rally, sometimes you can do it with a return of serve, but the most dramatic form is approaching the net. Still another great way to pressure your opponent's time and space is to bring them to the net on your terms. The speed or the location of your shot can pressure your opponent. Your movement forward changing the tempo of the rally can also put pressure on your opponent. Your forward movement can also have the effect of shrinking the space that your opponent can hit past you. In this chapter we will mainly focus on the serve and rally aspects of taking time away from your opponent.

You can use your serve to take away time and space, since the shortest distance between two points is a straight line, your serve will arrive faster to your opponent when you hit it right at them.

Tactics: Pressure Opponent's Time and Space

This pressures your opponent in two ways. One, they have less time to react because the distance is shorter. Two, you force them to make a decision very quickly as to whether to take it as a forehand or backhand and then also to pick to which target they want to hit. Advanced players can serve to either side of the line of decision and thus force the opponent to make tougher decisions. If your serve is too slow or it always goes slightly to the forehand side, this will not be as effective as faster serves that are directed at the body.

Another benefit of serving into the body, is that you cause you opponent to first respect and maybe fear that serve, which can leave them slightly hesitant to move to corner balls, because they worry about the body serve. This way you can be more effective with serves wide or down the middle of the court. A word of caution is that some players are very well trained to get out of the way of the ball hit at them moving to hit a big forehand.

#

Subtle and Obvious Change in Your Position to Take Away Time and Space

I have heard it said, "playing aggressively does not necessarily mean hitting hard, it means moving forward". On return of serve, standing at the baseline, or even slightly inside the baseline can give you the opportunity to put your opponent under time pressure, but that is predicated on how good the incoming serve might be. You may even find yourself inching in closer to the net. Caution: No matter how weak your opponent's serve is, I never recommend standing any further forward than halfway inside the large rectangle behind the service line. If you are too close to the service box, you are in danger of being pushed back by the serve, if it lands deep in the service box.

There was a junior player I trained for a while and I would test his ability to understand the game. He and I would play points, and I would ask him questions about the pivotal moment in a point where it was won, lost, or something took control of it. In an attempt to help him discover how to put time pressure on an opponent: I would rally a few balls back, then I would quickly step forward a few feet for the next ball, changing the rhythm of the rally, putting him under a subtle time pressure. He would them miss his shot or hit something weak for me to capitalize on for an attack. After the point I would ask him "What happened in that point?" He had a number of answers as I continued to use this same tactic against him. He felt he had done something wrong. When I explained that I had changed the rhythm of the rally and that he should look to see if I had changed my position, as that would affect the amount of time he would have to recover for his next shot. Once he made the adjustment, it was much more difficult for me to victimize him with that tactic. He then was better able to defend, but he used the same tactic against me and others.

#

Approaching the Net:

Best Time and Space Pressure Move

Coming to the net can be simple or it can be complex. The more you work on your technique and make your trips to the net a complex problem for your opponent, the better off you will be. At the very least If you learn to hit a low and deep approach shot and can come forward for one good volley to finish a point, then you have enough net game to pressure your opponent. Up to a 4.0 level of play you either need a very good approach shot, or a very good volley. Once you want to climb to 4.5 and above and want to play the net, you must have a very good approach and volley, and the ability to hit more than one volley to win the point. Also, when you have a reliable overhead, then your confidence at the net will soar.

Let's cover some of the basics of coming to the net. First, come in on a ball that would be easy to run forward immediately after hitting the ball. If hitting the approach shot forces you to really stop or even move back slightly, it's not the right ball for you to come to the net. Also the incoming ball should not pull you off balance or a be a ball that you may have trouble controlling. Your goal is to hit a ball deep down the line, and move right inside the service line. Again, see a coach for the specifics of what is realistic for you and your game.

I define a deep ball as one that lands in the second half of the large rectangle, so essentially in the last nine feet of the court. You don't have to hit the baseline, although the closer it goes to the baseline, the better of an approach it will be. Additionally if its fairly close to the sideline on your down the line shot, that's great, but it's far more important for it to be deep.

When approaching on your forehand side, I recommend hitting the ball with a minimal amount of topspin, just enough for it to land it, but not so much that it lands short and jumps up. Less topspin will not only help you gain more depth in the court, but give you a lower ball with more speed, all of which together puts more pressure on your opponent. You may also accidentally hit a winner, or force an error outright from your opponent, either of those is great, but continue to be ready to volley. Too many times in my life I have seen players come to the net, believing that their approach was too good and the opponent will not get there, they relax. The opponent then returns the ball and because the approaching player lost focus for a moment, they miss the volley. So be sure that you are there, present and ready, for anything until you are certain the point is over.

Coming the net suddenly forces your opponent to have to hit a great shot, immediately. Even if in the short term the opponent can handle that, over time the repeated challenge can wear them down and have a cumulative effect of pressure on them. Additionally, a passing shot thats easy at 15-love for them, becomes much more difficult for them when a game or set is on the line. While I don't necessarily prescribe to 'playing according to the score', having a set play to apply more pressure on pivotal points can be a positive factor for success.

Before we wrap up this section, I want to include another tactic for pressuring the opponent's time and space, which is to bring your opponent to the net on your terms, not theirs. Some people you play seem allergic to the net, and will only come to the net to shake hands at the end of a match. Others love the net and want to come forward as much as they can, but on their terms.

#

Bringing the Opponent Up on Your Terms

Against the 'Net Allergen' player, you can hit intentionally very short shots that pull them forward off balance. Keep doing this until they are forced to come in and then pass them or lob them. This is easier said than done, but you can see that it would require your ability to control the depth of your shots and described in another strategy.

It may seem odd to bring the player who likes the net forward, but if you have them coming in on your terms, then they will not be as comfortable coming forward, and you can gain an edge. Here is the best example: Raymond, the #1 player at a high school where I was coaching, who had been a fairly high ranked junior and was about equivalent to a 4.0 level player, was facing a senior who had been all-league the year before and was bigger, faster, stronger, and loved coming to the net. Very early in the set Raymond found himself down a break, but he shifted his focus to making sure the net player had to stretch for the first volley, so that he could open up space on the other side for a passing shot. My player broke serve, and won a very narrow set in a tiebreaker. For the second set, Raymond focused on hitting short balls to the sides of the court, and not down the middle. The opponent was then forced to come in with a sort of zig zag movement which increased the distance and slowed him down due to the direction change necessary. Raymond broke serve twice in the set to win 6-3 and come out with a convincing win, from what may have been a very tight match, simply because he made the net player play according to his terms.

On the Day of the Match

Maybe you don't need to put pressure on your opponent's time and space to win today's match. That's OK, but sometimes it's the only way to make an impression on some types of players. Be sure to take a few balls early by stepping inside the court to time your shot properly. Attempting to execute this strategy without practicing the timing on the court surface on which you are playing the match today can lead to some unnecessary errors.

Mental Skills: Pressuring Time and Space

When coming forward, be the aggressor, take charge of the point. Be ready to roll the dice, gamble and win 65% or more of the points. Maybe coming to the net is your only way to win 50% or more of the points, so be ready continue. As for bringing the other player up, be mentally prepared to hit softer lower shots that land around the service line or even a bit shorter. This is a great reason to warm up in the short court to practice those types of placements. Also, realize that when you shift to this strategy in a match, you might make an error or two in the early going as you figure out the timing of the shot

Break Up Your Opponent's Rhythm

Bill Tilden in "Match Play and Spin of the Ball" said, something to the effect of "Every ball should be struck with some type of intentional spin". So whether you choose to hit the ball with nearly the exact spin every time, or go for a very wide variety of spins, if you do so intentionally then you have it nailed. Your intention should be based on what you see in your opponent. However, if you have not thought much about this then you are missing out on a very effective strategy that can change the outcome of a match. Tilden also said "Find out which shot your opponent hates the most... and know which shot is your opponent's favorite", again I am paraphrasing. Once you know your opponent's least favorite shot, whether its high topspin, low slice, or a very fast flat ball with almost no spin, you can use that knowledge to set chances to hit that way when you really want a point, especially if you are down in a game, or have a game point. Knowing the opponent's strength helps you to avoid it, and it might be that they love when you give them just enough spin so they can take it at a certain height. I know that for my own game, when players hit me a certain amount of topspin, that allowed me to tee off on my groundstrokes, hitting more winners. HIgher or lower, and I would have to work my way to net in order be be more effective. If you can spin it differently to give the opponent a ball higher, lower, wider, or tighter to their body to take them away from their ideal contact point, you can greatly diminish their effectiveness. Make sure you are comfortable and confident with all the spins, before you decide to try them in a match for the first time

Here are a few combinations I like:

1. Slice shot that elicits a short return, followed by a heavy topspin angled shot.
2. Varying topspin, slice, topspin shots can get your opponent out of rhythm.
3. A variety of topspins heavy, medium, to almost flat, to change the way the ball 'jumps' to the opponent. Also when hitting topspin you can attack

the balls from different angles to create subtle differences in how the ball jumps.
4. Hitting no two shots alike can really wreck your opponent's rhythm. More on that later.
5. Serve with different types of spin by attacking the ball at different angles.
6. Serves that are spun above the 45 degree plane, or from 7 o'clock to 1 o'clock will have a very different effect than a ball struck at 8 o'clock to 2 o'clock. See a seasoned Tennis Professional if this is not clear to you. This not so subtle change is due to the difference in how the bottom of the ball is spinning when it makes contact with the ground.

If you use spin expertly, you can convince your opponent that they are having a bad day. Sadly, you may not gain acknowledgement for having played well, your opponent, their coaches and family will blame them for losing, while you know the real truth.

#

On the Day of the Match

Figure out which spin you want to start with in your warm up. Find a way that works for you. I like to start with moderate topspin, then slice, then alternate slice and topspin. From there Hit a moderate topspin, followed by heavy topspin and minimal topspin, just enough to keep the ball in the court.

Mental Skill: Disrupting Rhythm

Acceptance of a few errors will be important if you are going to change up your spins quite often. You will have to accept a few miss hits, and some occasional bad choices, and some ineffective shots. First, accept your error, then quickly think about how you can do better then next time in that same situation.

Power: the Final Strategy to Master, unless... Simple tactics for the power game

If you are going to be a power player, then you must work very hard to have impeccable timing on a wide variety of shots coming your way. I have seen Andre Agassi's coach working with him and giving Agassi every kind of ball imaginable. Agassi hit them all very hard, relentlessly. On the other hand you will also need to be able to play some defensive shots, because when you give your opponent power to work with, then they will also hit some offensive shots. You will want to be able to neutralize their powerful shot with a nice slice, a lob or a looping shot, before you go right back on the attack.

On the Day of the Match

Set the tone early. By the end of your pre-match warm up you will want to be hitting the ball confidently as hard as you can with 'controlled aggression'. All the power in the world will not help you if your ball is out.

Set the tone in the match. Hit the first serve of the match as hard as you can, if it goes in, do it again, if you are serving out of your mind, keep going. I have had players play magically on a given day and simply pummel the other player into oblivion, this is not a time for thinking. Carry on! However, if you miss that first serve, or you get derailed from your power game plan, consider adding some spin to your shots to keep them in, but only apply enough spin, so that you don't completely lose your aggression. Should spin not help, then you can focus on keeping the ball deep, being very patient and waiting for a short ball before becoming aggressive again. If that's not working hit some deep/short, short/deep combinations to elicit a weak reply. Do you see where I am headed? If you have built your power game on top of these foundations that come first, then if your power game is off for a day, you can fall back on other tactics and still find yourself with opportunities to finish points with power. With no foundation previous, I guess you just have a bad day and lose. So...

If all else fails focus on deep crosscourt, and it really may come back to simply running around and making one more shot. Let's hope it never comes back to that.

Mental Skill: Power Tennis

Commitment to your game plan and your development as a power player means you stay committed to it as your "A game" even if you make a few consecutive errors, but if you find yourself down a set and a break, then you may consider a strategic shift. However, do not abandon your game plan simply because you made a few errors, even a few in a row. Power Tennis means higher risk, and you have to continue taking risks to play your game.

The Best and Most Tiring Ways to Win

The best way to win is to overpower your opponent. It can also be the easiest way to lose. Sometimes even in a warm up you can see that your opponent can't handle your power. So play powerfully. It's the best way to win, because the points are shorter, and you expend less energy in winning the match, unless you fail to play with controlled aggression, because then you will make an inordinate amount of errors, making things more difficult for yourself. So, if you are winning games easily, continue on, but if you have a second match on the day, and you are making more than 2 errors per game, and games are going to deuce, you may want to play slightly differently.

This completely backfires, when power feeds right into your opponents' strengths, they love pace, and have a way of beating you with it. Also, if you are getting overpowered and are losing a set, either ramp it up, or switch to another mode of play. Some players will use all of the pace you provide, and simply return it with none, or turn it into massive spin.

Second best way to win is to keep your opponent under constant pressure to move. Using shot combinations that rarely allow your opponent to set up for their shot on time and in balance, will feed you a steady stream of weaker shots, and you can build your game on attacking in various ways the short or floating balls that come your way. I recommend that you build the strength of your point on crosscourt play, going for greater angles when the opportunity arises. If you continue to build your points with initial crosscourt shots, your opponent will move more and you will move less.

Time pressure with court position and change of pace. When you move forward or intentionally hit a slightly faster ball in a rally, you can take over the point. Sometimes this is subtle and sometimes not very subtle at all. Generally it's true that if your opponent is much faster on court than you, it will be good for you to move a bit closer in to keep them under time pressure. Faster opponents generally do not feel a lot of movement pressure, so you want to instead take away their time. This can also include coming to the net occasionally.

Disrupting the opponents rhythm can work to support one of the three above strategies. Either you can use this strategy over the course of a full match, or you can use it as a way to get your opponent off their game until you can return to your own "A game". Sometimes you play a someone who loves this type of play, and they will quickly use it against you by playing it better. Some people really love to be very creative with their shot making and the more you junk things up, the more you play into their hands so be careful.

On a day when all else has failed, running around hitting one more ball in the court can win you a match. Through sheer will and competitive instincts, counterpunching through a match to win can be very courageous. As a way of life, or a career, it can lead to injury, and overuse. Every match will be difficult. You will find it harder and hard to put opponents away. Those will more aggressive games will always have a chance of being ON, and can beat you when they play in the zone. You however will rarely if ever beat yourself. I strongly recommend that you begin to branch out and work to develop some of the skills shown above so that this will someday be your B or C game. There have been times as a player and a coach, that all else was failing and the only chance of winning was to run 6 miles for the victory. You have to do what you have to do!

When to Change Strategy and What to Expect

Strategic shifts are not easy to pull off, as there is a period of adjustment. So whether you are using your A game or B game, you might want to pick the one that you believe has the best chance against today's opponent. Winning on the day and in the match is always the most important consideration of the day, using all the tools at your disposal. When making a shift toward building more tools in your game, in the short term you will find that you lose a match that you may have won previously. When you manage it best, you can experience those losses in a practice match situation, and not a live tournament or team match situation. One of the lost pieces in the over programming of a tennis player is that practice match, or a friendly match just for the love of the game.

How to Build New Strategy into your Game

I often tell my students that there are five steps to truly building a new stroking weapon, or tactic to support a strategy.

Step One: Take a Lesson on the technique or tactic. There may be some closed skill drilling, and some repetitive drilling.
Step Two: Live ball drilling featuring that same skill or tactic.
Step Three: Point play competition where the skill or tactic is required or rewarded.
Step Four: Practice matches where the tactic or technique is stressed much more than the winning of the match. Wait until confidence and mastery come about before using it in...
Step Five: using what you have learned in a lesser tournament, so that you can decide whether you will also use it against the best competition you will face.

Now that you have fully bought into this progression as a framework, I hope you are not disappointed when I turn them on their head. I hope you understand that in order to climb to the top of game and do what is best, you need other supporting structures based on smart Tennis. So now, let's turn this thing completely upside down. From this list of five ways to win, I hope you have one strong one match strategy, in which you are very confident, and two others that you are comfortable in playing. If you can play all five, you will be quite successful, be careful not to overthink your matches.

Developing a Long Term Approach to Playing Style

Wherever you find yourself along this continuum of playing styles, it's wise to be thoughtful about your plan for the future of your game. What will you need to become to play the way you want to play? My own transformation from counterpunching baseline player to full time serve and volleyer happened overnight. Only on very special days where my opponent was overmatched or hitting right into my wheel house, did I ever play a power game. I did however rack up more wins than losses against players more powerful than myself, by using all the guile described in these pages. Even more importantly, the players I have coached have benefitted greatly from the fact that I learned from past mistakes so that I could help them at a younger age find their A, B and maybe their C game. My hope is that you will experience the great fun that comes from using sound strategies and find similar or better success than my people.

This ends this section on basic strategy. My goal with this is to give you a sample of the foundation upon which the rest of the books will be built, including the print book which will be ready in early 2015.

Top 5 Mental and Emotional Foundations
for Winning Tennis

#

Introduction

The goal of this book is to provide a fairly unique framework for developing as close to an ideal environment for your training and development as a tennis player. Your environment is internal and external. Your Mind, Body, and Emotions can all work together to help keep you on task as a buoyant competitor. As it says in the title, these are mental and emotional foundations on which you can build. We must of course include the Mind/Body/Emotional connection, because they are all connected and can postively or negatively influence each other.

What you will find in this book comes from 26 years of experience of applying the principles learned through reading as well as conferences with other tennis professionals throughout the years to find the precise mix of that has worked so well for myself and my players. While some of the themes may seem familiar to those who have studied the application of sports psychology, you may personally find a unique application of those principles in this book. For players, coaches and parents to truly be working collaboratively in cohesion with the player's best interest, discussion of the following material could prove to be extremely valuable.

The unique framework of this book is that it builds on what ought to be obvious, but sometimes is not so clear. The book begins by examining why someone would want to play tennis. When we begin by questioning all assumptions, then we have an opportunity to truly understand what the deeper motives are behind playing the game, and we can then move on to a discussion of goals, values and motivation. The player's values act like a sort of true north on a compass, helping the player to continue to move in the direction that they want. Setting the compass in the direction that we would like to go allows for better ability to make course corrections along the way as adversity arises. Every player must overcome some type of adversity on the way to playing at their best level.

Many of the other decisions that need to be made by a player in regard to their attitudes about coaching, how they go about their work, and what type of image they want to project will fall in line with these values that were created, which act as a type of moral compass. A player's attitude about competition, how coachable they will be, and the ability to adapt and change will be determined by their values.

In short, this book is about becoming a great tennis player by creating the best possible environment both internally and externally.

#

Knowing for whom you play

I had an interesting chat with a national expert on physical education and athletics. He is a university professor, an author of many books, and a much sought after speaker. In our discussion in regard to one of my other books, "Playing Sports Right: Your Way", he shared that the vast majority of athletes playing at his well-noted Division 1 school were still playing to please their parents. He engages them in conversation and is vitally interested in getting to know them as people, since many of them are his students in the Kinesiology/Physical Education department. It seemed to weigh heavily on him that very few he saw played for the pure unbridled love of the sport for their own enjoyment, and that many of them felt quite a bit of internal pressure to please others in their performance. Whether they are playing to please parents or coaches, or if you or I are doing the same, it is not ideal when attempting to create the best possible environment for the best performances.

Sometimes the environment has been created by the people who oversee it, and many times it's an internal choice of the player. When coaching young athletes, I have consistently sent the message, "If you want to play to try to please me, you need to know that I am always pleased. Of course if you fail to give the best effort level, or you fail to learn, then I may be disappointed in the short term. However, you never need to fear me, simply because you lost." As a practical aside on this, I underline my words with actions. One promise I make to my teams is whether we win or lose, after our toughest match, or toughest stretch in the season, we will have a 'game day' where we play nothing but fun games, and there will be no conditioning. The opposite of that would be to threaten, or change my mind and break my promise to them.

I made a conscious decision that I wanted to play tennis because it's what I wanted to do and not to please anyone, or prove anything except to myself. What may be of interest is that my decision came at the age of 23. Part of the magic of being a champion coach has been my ability to allow players to play for joy, and allowing them to play for me, but letting them know that no matter what they do I am pleased. Also, some decide to play for a higher power, like Michael Chang. So, take a moment and say to yourself "I am playing because I love this sport", or whatever words you want to use to make it YOURS.

Later, we may need or want to play for a team. Playing on a team can be a true joy and honor, provided you retain your love of the game. Perhaps it's a dramatic Hollywood depiction, but from the movie Miracle in which the 1980 Men's Hockey team performed the Miracle on Ice, the coach drew out of the team the concept of "Who do you play for?" Of course the answer was, "My name is Mike Eruzione, and I play for the United States of America", with the point being that the one player who emerged as a leader was the first to understand the mission. Tennis is interesting because it is one of the few individual sports that is also often combined into a team sport at the high school, college and recreational levels.

In my Master's program in Education, there was a phrase that has stayed with me, which has a bearing in regard to our sports culture. "Everyone is influenced by their culture, but no one is bound by it". As we have increasingly become a multicultural society which is more of a salad bowl than the melting pot of previous years, we find a certain culture clash when it comes to differing values in the mix of fun, recreation, sports and the meaning of competition. It is a great idea to stop, reflect and decide on what you want to build upon in your tennis life.

Values and Goals

If you are going to create your best playing level, you need to set some goals. One thing I have learned recently, that I wish I had clued into much earlier is the art of aligning my goals with my values. Had I known how powerful that would be, I would have done it much earlier. I vaguely remember pushing past that part of the process in the past, not seeing how it might help.

Not long ago, I went through a process during which I clarified my values, and was astonished in regard to how much more empowering that was for me. I then was able to write my objectives with much more clarity. Once my objectives were established, my goals seemed to write themselves. The goals then made better sense to me. Previously goal setting had scared me, not because I was afraid of a challenge, but I had failed to connect those goals to the reasons why was worthwhile to pursue them. Before clarifying my values I felt I could only write a few goals. But now I found I could write many more goals and found them to be not very frightening at all, because I could see that if any goal affirmed all five of my stated values, then it was central to my life. If a goal affirmed four values, it was still a very strong part of my priorities. I then prioritized my goals based on number of values affirmed, and I have had a much more rich experience with goal setting as a result. One of the great results has been the writing of books to help the tennis community to grow stronger! Join my email list, and I will send you a values exercise to get you started! You may also be very interested in this particular book 5 Secrets of Goal Setting as I found it to be a revelation for my own goal setting process.

As it pertains to your values, I strongly recommend that you discover your reasons for competing. Why do you do it? Once you discover what you value from the experience, then it's quite possible you may become a much more empowered competitor.

Two Lines of Competitive Logic

There are two main segments of logic that run through the sporting world. When someone can suggest another line of logic, I will include it in future additions.

Line of Logic 1:

Tennis is a sport. Sports are competition. Competition has winners and losers. If you win, you are a winner and if you lose you are a loser. Winners are celebrated. Losers should try harder to become, winners. This is a fairly common and not very nice line of logic. Here participation is diminished.

Line of Logic 2:

Tennis is a sport. Sports are competition. Competition is a game. Games are something people play. Playing is fun.

There are many great stories of athletes who discovered the true joy of playing, and thus became champions in sport and life.

At the core of competition is cooperation, because two players must come together cooperatively to discover who is better on the day and deserves to move onto the next round. The word competition comes from the latin root competere which means “Two seeking together”. By that definition competition really requires a certain level of cooperation in order for a game to be played.

So engage the competition well, according to your values, and honor those who engage with you and their values even if they differ.

#

Fear, Pressure, Despair

“Courage is resistance to fear, mastery of fear--not absence of fear. Except a creature be part coward, it is not a compliment to say he is brave; it is merely a loose misapplication of the word.” ~ Mark Twain

Now if you have established your values objectives and goals, most of the framework for defeating fear pressure and despair has been established. Every athlete experiences fear and/or pressure to succeed at times. The question then arises, if you play for the love of the game, what is it that has you experiencing fear? If you've made the big decisions about which direction you want to move, then what is the source of fear and pressure? It could be a lingering thought or feeling. The same question may be applied to the experience of pressure on court. If you are playing only for your own enjoyment, are their other reasons that have you feeling pressure? Do you have a need to be #1 and anything less than that is dissatisfying? It can be hard to enjoy your game, and play your game well under those kinds of internal pressure.
In order to create a near ideal training environment, identifying the sources of fear and overcoming or eliminating them is a project in and of itself.

Everyone brings some element of fear to their competitive lives. Linda LeClaire and her husband Dr. Bryce Young are experts in the field of helping athletes play with confidence, understand and become more free of fear in their athletic lives. I would encourage anyone to reach out to them. I found that recognizing my own fears as an athlete helped me not only to come to terms with them, but to see how my athletes fears differed from my own. It's great to have strategies to mitigate fear, especially when hitting a second serve at break point in the second, if already down a set.

Pressurizing and excuse making thoughts many times contain the words Would, Could or Should. Although there is not a hard and fast rule that can be written

You might not be able to completely eliminate these words from your life, as that would create some fairly awkward communication, but you could examine how you think and speak and you should best form your thoughts.

Here are examples of when those words can become a problem. "You should have won that match!" "I would have won that match, if..." "I could have won, if I had tried". Using the word 'could' sounds so very hopeful, as thought the next time around in the same circumstance the outcome will be different. However, it is really a form of excuse making. The message that is delivered is that if all the conditions had been favorable, then I will be able to do my best. If I am unable to do my best, then I have an excuse for failing.

I 'would have' is similar to 'could have', but is more advanced in excuse making, because of the higher level of certainty in the players mind that the outcome would change.

I or you 'should have' is an extreme pressure word and many times it comes from outside the player. "You should have won that match". The additional connotation of the thought is that there is some shame assigned for failing, when success was supposedly easily within reach. This of course discounts the ability and determination of the opponent, and also takes the focus away from what happened in the match. What can be learned about the performance that can be different the next time. The fact that some type of shame is being assigned to the outcome makes it more difficult for the player to take an objective view of what happened in that match.

When you learn to put these kinds of thoughts away, then you can take a more rational view of what happened, and begin to plan more a process oriented approach to future matches.

#

Specific Goal Setting Ideas

When setting goals for your tennis performance, it's best to start with the largest goals first. Depending on where you are in your development you may want to choose between:1. five year 2. three-year and, 3. possibly only one year worth of goals. Younger, newer players may want to plan one year at a time, and older more ambitious players may want to start with a five-year plan. When setting these larger goals it's okay to have some outcome goals in terms of ranking levels, however it may be more valuable to create more performance goals and process goals. Performance goals may include attaining a certain level of velocity on a stroke, a certain amount of foot speed, overall fitness levels, or any area of performance that can be measured. Process oriented goals may relate to the schedule of training, the qualities of game style to be developed, and others somewhat subjective areas of character development that need to be improved for complete preparation for future success.

One of my favorite outcome goals is to find a small group of players or a team that you can identify that he would like to beat or that your team would defeat. As an individual player if you were to pick up 3 to 5 players who you consider benchmarks for reaching a certain developmental plateau. You can write their names on the 3 x 5 card or a yellow sticky or a piece of tape, placing that somewhere you can see it every day. When I coach a team I instruct my players to put the name of a certain team on a 3 x 5 card, placing it somewhere visible, so that we together have a goal of defeating a certain team in league or in playoff action.

Sometimes, I keep my own outcome goals a secret. I will never forget the time I wrote on my calendar at the beginning of the year to beat a certain team. I then called that coach to set up a match. When the coach did not respond immediately I began to I continue to follow up with them up until one week left before the season started, which meant it was now too late to schedule a match with them. This meant that the only way we would play that game would be in sectional playoffs. Given the remote possibility that we would face them in the playoffs I did not feel so good about looking at the name of that team on my calendar, but I did keep the name there for the entire season. In a "truth is stranger than fiction" story, that should only appear in a story book, my team met that team in the championship game of the sectional playoffs. Facing the three to one match deficit on a 97° day my determination to win that match was never greater. My team, which had no knowledge of the fact that I had made this goal for myself at the beginning of the season, responded incredibly to the adversity of being behind needing to win the final four sets on court, doing just that. They were crowned section champions. I have never shared with them my outcome goal for their performance.

I did however share with them performance goals in relation to running drills to be performed under a certain threshold of time. I did share with them an expectation that what first serve percentage. Additionally, it became quite clear to them that I never wanted to see a serve go into the net. These are just a few of the performance goals that I have used with my high school tennis teams.

In relation to process goals I expressed to all my players, that I expected everyone to become more intelligent in their tactics and to become mentally stronger in their approach to the competition. Those types of outcomes are not so easily measured, but I can share with great confidence that by and large the majority of our players improve dramatically in their own understanding of strategy and tactics as well as their own mental strategies for their particular personalities and game styles.

Game Exposure, Fear of Change... Cooperation!

If you love the game, and want to improve dramatically, then every once in a while your game will need to be exposed to very high levels of competition. At that time, you have a choice. Do you want your game to be exposed? Having your game exposed is the surest way to find out what you need to learn. Then you will be required to change for the better, or whither. Most every top player is constantly working to improve to prolong their career in every sport, including Tennis. The work ethic of a professional athlete is a great model for any type of success in life. When Federer had his time of dominance he had improved beyond every other player, and there was a distance between he and second place. But then his main challangers improved in important ways. Novak Djokovic became perhaps the best server returner, rivaling the best ever in the game. Rafa Nadal developed a stronger serve and more penetrating groundstrokes. Andy Murray developed a stronger forehand and a net game to use to mix up his tactics. Every sport in the world is played at a higher level of performance every progressive year. The emergence of sports science, and performance psychology have helped athletes to attain more and more levels of speed, balance, strength than ever before, while also fine tuning their mental skills. Equipment has allowed for greater amounts of speed. The game is really all about how well do you improve, not how good are you right now.

THE BEST WAY TO IMPROVE IS...

TO HAVE YOUR GAME EXPOSED!

Losing in the short run, may help you more than having a 90% winning record. Knowing that you have an opponent who understands your weakness and how to exploit it, can motivate you to improve your areas of relative weakness, and use your strengths in new ways. How else will you gain the motivation to work on your weaknesses, unless you know you are doomed unless you do. For the sake of confidence many coaches recommend that you maintain a 50% or greater winning percentage. You can easily manage that by selecting the level of tournaments you play very carefully. Once you have a winning percentage that begins to climb above 75% over a period of a few months, then you will want to increase the challenge level of the events you play.

If you want to play at a high level you need every shot, and its more important to have your weaknesses exposed and shore them up than it is to develop strengths. Limiting weaknesses gives your game staying power. I can think of two examples of players who had a relative weakness, solved it and rose in the rankings. Chris Evert had been exposed by Martina Navratilova as being less fit, possessing less power and lacking weapons with which to beat Martina. Chris had always relied on steady shot making and accuracy. Martina changed the way the women's game was played. Chris Evert adapted and did all that she needed to do to retake the #1 ranking, becoming more fit, improving her balance, adding power and more net play to her own game.

Jim Courier seemed stuck at #9 in the world. In a famous quote at the time he said "I'm 20 years old, I'm Number 9 in the world, and I'm so unhappy with my life!" I was reminded that among Pete Sampras, Andre Agassi, Michael Chang and Jim, that Courier was first to #1 in the world, but seems to be overlooked. It also seemed that when Courier could not break through at #9, that he finally began to apply some of the lessons learned from Jose Higueres, in addition he added some speed to his serve. When Courier, like Evert, also added the factor of coming to the net to finish points now and then that he rose to #1. He had been strictly a baseline threat, and was working too hard for every point. Coming up to net to close out a point a bit sooner finish now and then gave his opponents more to think about and also helped him to save energy over the course of a match, or even a tournament.

#

Accepting Phases of Change

When we need to leave a place or a way of being, it can feel like dying. When people die there are stages of grieving that people go through, and in our sporting lives it can be small death to make a major change in our approach. We get **Angry**, We Face **Denial**, **Negotiate**, Feel **Guilt and Shame**, and finally we get to a place of **Acceptance**. I hope that no matter what age you are, you will always accept that change is inevitable and continue to work on improving something in your game. I hear a lot of talk about how American teenagers are avoiding playing one another for fear of exposure, which would mean they would have to change their game. Apparently in Spain, promising 13-15 year old players are required to play a low level professional event. This exposes their game, and becomes a time of decision. If they are beaten soundly and then still have a strong desire to close the gap between their current ability and world class play, then it will become readily apparent. I would hope that there is also a support structure in place to help guide this process. Players who are more or less coddled, don't seem to respond as well on the big stage later in life.

Plateaus in your game are actually helpful, so that you can learn to cope with your new level. If you dramatically improved every day, it would become very stressful on your system. It's very stressful to be under constant change, because our minds are not set up to cope with uncertainty, so when you do attain a new level, be happy to get used to that new level before climbing higher.

There are also times in training when it is ideal not to change. Shortly before high level events, you want to be settled and dialed into exactly how you want to play. If on the day before a big match, you feel you are doing to build a new skill into your game, you are probably dreaming. It's not likely to happen. On the other hand if you practice a stroke that you own, but had let you down in a previous match, you are probably on the right track.

You and your team want to make a periodized schedule of training that will allow for periods of significant change, adjustment, fine tuning and finally being fully prepared in competition for further levels of competition.

#

Build Trust and Cooperation with Peers

A player gains a huge advantage in training when they can practice with a wide variety of practice partners at the same level, a higher level and a lower level. Many coaches agree that a player is best advised to practice 60% to 75% of the time with players who are a similar level, the remaining 25% to 40% can be spent practicing with players at different levels, higher and lower. Higher level players might not want to practice for long periods of time with you, so maximize the time. Build up your karmic energy by also practicing with lower level players and have specific objectives to work on while doing so.

At all times and as much as it depends on you, make friends. Even when you are not making a friend, you can still find suitable practice partners who join together simply to be of mutual benefit to one another. Over the course of the last few years, I have heard many high level coaches bemoaning the fact that juniors are not playing enough practice matches.

Therefore, avoid alienating your local peers. Be quick to admit a mistake, be quick to forgive the mistakes of others. Embrace a spirit of cooperation. Even if you might not really like someone as a friend, as long as you can come to an agreement about how to practice and maintain a somewhat equal relationship of working on what they other wants to work, then you are best advised to seek out those practice partners. Sometimes that will offer a more focused and profitable time of practice since the social aspect is nearly eliminated.

Similarly, if a player has depended on cheating, intimidation, or other forms of gamesmanship to gain and edge, the advantage gained with those ploys will quickly go away when playing at a Division 1 college level or higher when many more matches are officiated. Those players will often find it very difficult to find suitable practice partners, as almost anyone may rather associate with a lesser player than to be be associated with a known cheater. Just the same you can attempt to befriend that person, and it could be you that helps liberate them from the dark place of isolation, cheating and the 'Me against the world' attitude.

When players rise to a certain level where more matches are officiated and calls are corrected, then real exposure of a lack of character takes place. So even though you may lose more in the early days of your career, the fact that you did not take the easy road will help you when the bright lights are on, and every can see how you are. I sometimes see players who are playing an officiated match, and they seem helpless because they really want to be able to call a ball on the line out, but they can't, because its not in their hands. Ironically, it is commonplace that you may play someone in their hometown, with their hometown official watching the match, and things might not at all go your way. This happens in every country of the world, and more often in some countries. You won't know until you get there, but if you aspire to move through the various levels of minor league pro level events, you will see for yourself. In the long run for the longer term strategy of success take the more principled rout, and it will pay off for you more in the future.

Maximum Fitness and Performance

There is no way for one book to reach all players, due to the wide variety of body types, personalities, training environments and the level of access to equipment and expertise that each player has available to them. This section acts more as a guide than the final say on these items. I will give some general advice, but you will be best advised to stay current on all the latest techniques in training or hire someone who is well aware of them.

When you train your body, the most important priorities are to build up your highest performance threshold, injury prevention, and overall health. Maintaining a balance of all three of the above is very important, as some people work past the point of pain, injury or exhaustion in pursuit of a high performance threshold. Pushing too hard too fast to increase that threshold exposes you to injury, both acute and chronic.

Be sure to discover best practices and choose wisely where there are types of training that are controversial. An example of training that is controversial, but only in a small corner of the athletic training world is the debate in regard to unstable surface training with Bosu Balls and similar pieces of equipment. Unstable surfaces and the like are great at helping develop better which may create greater stability in joints. Some research shows that unstable surface training may hinder your mobility, thus damaging your speed and flexibility.

Over training in any regard can damage your overall health. Our bodies need adequate rest in order to recover, and then build on that work. An analogy for understanding this is the four seasons, and day and night. If we only had Summer, then their would be no vegetation. Yes, we need a Winter in our training. For a primer on world class athletic training, be sure to listen to my interview with Alistair McCaw who has worked with many top tennis players as their fitness guru. A great athletic trainer listens to and observes their athlete very closely. If you are overtraining, you may find you wake up feeling more tired than usual, and/or feel lethargic during the day, while also experiencing the feelings of a low grade fever.

Think about Aesop's Fable "The Tortoise and the Hare". Slow and steady wins the race! Another analogy I use for this to understand training yourself is to imagine pouring water out of a jug. If you turn the jug upside down with all the air bubbles going up, the water actually comes out more slowly, and there is a lot of wasted energy. However, a controlled pour with the jug tipped at an ideal angle for venting the air allows for the water to come out faster and with less wasted energy. So you can see that the action that on the face of it would appear to be slow, is actually fast.

#

An argument can be made that Tennis Players at the highest levels are among the very most talented athletes in the world. At the Olympics, Roger Federer received an amazing amount of attention from his fellow athletes, largely for that reason, but also due to his ambassador like personality. Conversely, there are studies that suggest that the vast majority of Tennis players are among the worst trained athletes in the world, just above those that bowl and play softball.

To move beyond 4.0 as a player, you may need to identify weaknesses in your athleticism, as most every player 4.5 and above is a fine athlete, and even more so at ever ensuing level of the game. Here are some aspects of your training you will want to consider.

Here are some key components to the qualities you may want to develop, and please do your own research, and always consult the proper experts before beginning a training program.

1. Core Strength - Transverse Stability and Mobility are paramount. These are phrased learned from Alistair McCaw one of the world's best athletic trainers. Find him on social media, he is a great resource.

2. Flexibility - Some of the greatest gains in performance can be found in developing a greater range of motion from which to move, bend, twist, etc. More power and easier movement ensues. In addition risk of injury is reduced. One of the classic books on the topic is 'Stretching' by Bob Anderson, and I am sure you can find many more resources.

3. Anaerobic Endurance - Are you ready to perform hundreds of 5-10 yard sprint/explosions? You never really get to full speed on a tennis court, but being able to fully, and efficiently accelerate on court is paramount to your success in a match, especially in longer matches.

4. Elastic / Functional Strength - Improving your strength in motion, while mimicking tennis movements can be extremely beneficial when done properly.

5. Court Speed Development - There are quite a few wacko options to try, and some of them might be dangerous, so again be careful.

5. Explosive Strength - A type of fitness that is best supervised fully by an expert, and only to be done after establishing a great foundation of all around fitness.

6. Balance - This could be #1 on the list.

7. Agility and Footwork - Having 'organized feet' that give you precise footwork is a major part of what will appear in the next book.

8. Ball Throwing Ability Overhand - Footballs, baseballs and even softballs work. I have heard many times that throwing a football is an ideal way to train shoulder stability at the same time as learning proper mechanics of throwing. Note: serving is NOT exactly like throwing a ball.

9. Joint Stability or Mobility - Some people are fairly immobile and need greater mobility, few people have hyper mobility and need to gain stability.

10. Proper Breathing - Learning to breathe deeply enough, and to regulate your breathing is a great physical skill that can help facilitate better mental and emotional states for performance.

#

Cross training Supporting Athletic Skills

Many analysts point out that among the top players in the game these days, a large percentage of them grew up on playing often on clay. Is that really the commonality to bring most the these top players together? Perhaps an even more significant effect is that most of the top players also played soccer. In becoming a better athlete, to complete the full range of skills that one needs for gross motor, fine motor and cognitive development of full body awareness and a nearly complete athletic skill set, cross training experiences are vital.

Some of the benefits of cross training are:

1. 1. A variety of activity breaks up the monotony of only playing Tennis.
2.
3. 2. Balancing out your musculature, using different muscles as Tennis can be very unbalanced toward the dominant hand.
4.
5. 3. Fun
6.
7. 4. Other sports skills help support tennis playing, creating a deeper level of thought about strategy and tactics.
8.
9. 5. Social Interaction

Soccer supports flexibility of movement, and the ability to read and react quickly to changing conditions of play. Whether or not soccer playing is a larger factor in success for tennis players than playing on clay, certainly a large percentage of top players have cross trained in this way. Having an understanding of eye/foot coordination will help tremendously in your ability to get in great position for a tennis ball, as truly your feet are the vehicles by which you transport the racket to the ball. The more precise you can be in positioning, the better tennis player you will be.

Basketball has similar movements to Tennis, especially when playing defense. The exception here is where you will defend a concave arc forward on a tennis court, you will defend a convex arc more often in basketball. On the other hand there will be times when you would need to move in the opposite direction. Doubles players can be helped by the interchange of positioning with teammates, learning to read react and reposition. The breaking down into a strong defensive position helps support a very similar ready position in Tennis. The way you move to a ball to prevent the player going past you is similar to moving to a ball prior to it going past you. The difference is the angle of attack.

Badminton has some similarities to Tennis, and mostly it would be the value of the understanding of shot combinations. An article was produced a number of years ago comparing Pete Sampras' serve to a badminton overhead, and they looked almost identical. Be careful with other racket sports, because different muscle groups are used, so you might not want to spend too much time playing them, but

Two Man Beach Volleyball is a fun way to become a more explosive athlete. The sand, the demands of movement, the ability to dive flat out on a soft surface help you to gain more overall body control, and thus can really help in those emergency situations when retrieving a ball that is almost out of reach. Two person volley ball is also a great training tool for doubles players and to support anyone who would like to play the net in tennis. Confidence going for overheads and high volleys improves as you gain the ability to control play above the net. The touch of bumping and setting are similar to some the actions behind low volleys, half volleys, and those times when a player hits a ball hard right at you and you need to stand your ground. Having practiced bumping a volleyball that came from a hit by a guy 6'6 and 230#, I can tell you that it might not have hurt as much as getting hit by an 80mph forehand, but it did help with overcoming the fear of an impact. Those sessions left me with raised welts on my forearms.

Baseball Catching and various forms of stopping a baseball can help you in many ways on a tennis court, these receiving skills are not practiced much by those who have specialized in Tennis at an early age. Throwing a ball is a great way to develop the coordination to later adapt for serving. Pitching a baseball brings an understanding of spins, speeds, locations and how to set up points, and keep your opponent off balance. Batting helps teach you to slow things down in your mind and simply read and react. It is a well known fact that Andre Agassi, one of the very best returners in the history of the game, (during his time he was said to be the best ever), would visit batting cages and routinely hit 95 MPH fastballs as though it was nothing.

Baseball players are fond of saying that hitting a baseball is the most difficult single skill in any sport, but returning a 140mph serve might be right up there. I remember when 140mph was guaranteed not to be returned, but in the last 10 years, more and more often if that serve is within one step of the returner, some of the better returners can handle that. It was about 10 years ago, I remember seeing a 141 mph serve returned and was amazed. Today, that amazement has worn off. Of course a serve at 115mph and well placed can be impossible to return, simply because of geometry.

Darts, Archery, Gun Range

The ability in your mind to find a target, and accurately deliver a projectile to a target and then mental calm to repeatedly do that is a task that can be practiced in the serene world of darts, archery, or a gun range. I prefer Darts, as there is more of a fine motor aspect to the training. Professional tennis players many times spend whole hours of practice on pinpoint placement of a certain shot. Part of the skill set of a junior player coming up, is developing the capacity to spend considerable time focusing on precision of shot, footwork, dynamic and variable amounts of spin, etc. Until you reach a level of discipline to execute those kinds of practices, it will be difficult to achieve a level higher than 5.0, much less a world class level.

Ultimate Frisbee
This may be one of the most difficult anaerobic sports, as the need to explode and while changing direction can be non-stop for a few minutes at a time.

Ball Room Dance, and other forms of dance that offer trained footwork patterns. Tom Stow, one of the all time great coaches, promoted ball room dance to his players as a way to develop better overall coordination, balance and footwork. My own tennis was helped dramatically by learning ball room dance, and it also made me highly sought out at certain parties and events.

#

Being Coachable

I've been very fortunate as a coach to have worked with some very coachable players. It can take a period of time to gain trust of the new player who comes to you, or when you become the coach of the team. Once that trust is established it's much easier for a player and coach to understand one another. One of the most coachable players that I've worked with in over 25 years in the sport tried to keep his injury a secret from me. When I discovered that he was hurt I could see that he was worried about how I might react. When I showed that I wasn't going to overreact to this situation, also that I cared about his physical condition more than the outcome of his match, then he began to trust me much more than he had previously. From that moment forward our trust was established and it made the communication between us flow much more efficiently. That player did not go out of his way to ask me questions and pick my brain and try to discover all of the knowledge that I had, but he did know that I had his health in perspective. You want to find a coach you can trust similarly. After this trust was established, I notices also that there was more open dialogue about the state of his recovery. Another player who I had that was very coachable also was quite curious about the many matters and would often ask me questions about my tennis knowledge in regard to the stroke strategies and other aspects of training that would help him to excel. I many times remember fondly the times of coaching those players.

On the other hand there are players who to resist almost any outside information coming towards them for whatever reason. It can be quite difficult as a coach to understand why someone would want to play sport and not remain open to every bit of information that could possibly help them. If you happen to be that kind of person, then I encourage you to be a bit more open minded to what your coaches have for you. I had a number of players that I coach who did not seem to listen at the critical time or their anxiety level prevented them from really hearing and acting what was being said. As a player reading this the question I would pose to you is are you going to be the coachable player? Do you go to practice or workouts with questions ready? Do you listen intently and get every moment of wisdom that you can from your coach? Foster a curious spirit, as that curiosity about the mysteries of how to play better tennis is a great trait for you moving forward as you create an environment for success in your own mind!

Part of what's so powerful about fostering your own curiosity is that you can show that you are intrinsically motivated to learn. Players who always need to be told by coaches or parents can appear to be only extrinsically motivated. My advice to you here is that you listen actively by asking questions and following up until you have full understanding of what coaches and parents expect. That level of communication will also be a tremendous life skill for you moving forward into the working world.

Early Specialization

I recommend doing your own research on whether Tennis is an early specialization sport for you. My general recommendation is that young children should play as many sports as they can on grass and other softer surfaces. Indoor basketball on a gym floor is much easier on joints and limbs that asphalt. Many misguided players begin specializing too young, then when they really want to excel, they cannot due to sore knees, injured spines, and overused ankles. So do not become solely a tennis player at age 6, but if you are going to play great tennis, then you will need to ramp up the level of competition beginning before age 12 for best success. Of course there are many stories of players who came along after age 12 to begin playing competitively who then become top 100 players in the world, but those are fairly rare. One thing they have in common is that they did have early exposure, and some reasonable amount of participation in the game prior to specializing.

Some notes about research to help you avoid the negative impacts of earlier specialization. I want you to take my word for this, as I learned these items second hand: 1. The Italian Soccer Federation produced a study that showed athletes who had early balance training were less likely to suffer catastrophic knee injuries. 2. The French Tennis Federation found that players 10 or younger who served while using full extension and began to do that prior to developmental completion of the shoulder joint were much more likely to have chronic shoulder injuries as teens. 3. A friend was training in Spain, and saw on Spanish TV a feature on the negative effects on the spine for players who learn topspin or kick serve too early, prior to the age of 15. The arching of the back led to compression of vertebrae and thus micro fractures in the spine of those players.

I had a young man who worked for me teaching tennis and he reached #5 in our section in the Boy's 18s, but by that time, he was almost completely burned out on tennis, felt a lot of pain, and in the critical moments at the end of a very high level high school tournament had nothing left in his tank. While representing his team, and sorely wanting to do well, he was beaten convincingly by a lower ranked player.

When considering how early to start and how much time to put in on asphalt, be sure to consider how you want it all to end. A very high percentage of players who do well up to the 14/under age division in a few years will quit the sport or be so burned out on the competition or the pain. Some would say “It’s a testing ground to see how badly you want it!” I say it’s poor management. Your body is your only real resource as a player, take good care!

Pre-Match Preparation Helps You to Succeed

"Failure to prepare is preparing to fail"

General George S. Patton

Preparation and readiness are mostly an antidote to fear, but they mostly are simple physical rituals that give you the best chance in your match. The goal of the preparation is to have your mind, body, and game ready to be at ideal concentration, readiness, and fine tuning to be on for the first shot of the warm up. How can you be ready if you have not experienced the surface you are playing? Are you truly ready if you don't know where the rest room is, and how you might find it if you needed an emergency rest room break? Using the restroom is like preparing for a long drive in the car with someone where you are expecting to have no stops along the way. How can you be ready if you are not familiar with your surroundings? Ideas vary in regard to how much preparation you need prior to a match. I strongly recommend arriving on site between 30-45 minutes prior to your match. Walk around and see where all the courts are, look for issues on different courts: is there shade? cracks or other problems on the courts? Do some courts face differently? Do the courts face the best direction? How is the sun? Getting acclimated to all these things and just the simple familiarity with the site will have you feeling much more calm, than if you arrive just a few minutes prior to the start of your match. Plus, you can also watch a little Tennis, and that can help you prepare your mind. Since you want all of your mental energy to go into preparation for the match and not lose any portion to subconscious fears like "I feel like I could get lost in the club", or "If I need to use the rest room, I don't even know which way to go", "I am afraid of the unknown, what is the court going to look like when we get there?" "I wonder if I will know anyone at the tournament" "What if I suddenly see someone I know during the match, will I get distracted?" Arriving early can help you prepare mentally to answer all these questions. Additionally, you can also do things like skip rope, stretch and other activities to keep your ready physically, but you should most likely have already had some physical preparation prior to arrival.

Whatever you do, you need to balance the thought that you wont want to use up too much energy on the practice court, especially if you are scheduled for two matches in one day. In fact your mental and physical approaches may differ slightly depending on how many matches you have. Conversely if you are such a creature of habit that having precisely the same warm up regimen helps you then so be it.

This is ideal, as you can probably spend up to 20-30 minutes warming up your strokes, but there are more aspects to preparation than just the physical stroking part. So you will need to plan your warm up to give you enough time to still arrive at the site early enough. As a high school coach with 24 seasons experience, my routine for a 3:30pm start time was that I expected every player to be on court hitting by 3pm. Of course that would mean they would have to arrive some time before that, so they can park, walk, talk to their friends for a moment, and get their equipment situated. At 3pm if anyone was not on court, I would hurry them along, and at 3:05pm anyone who was not hitting would be urged to begin immediately. Precisely at 3:20pm, I would as everyone to serve for exactly 5 minutes, come together for a 5 minute pre-game talk, the proceed to introductions at 3:30pm. This routine helped us to be very strong starters in matches especially ready to serve well.

Are you fully alert? - Did you know it takes two full hours to wake up? So if you have an early morning match, be sure to get up at least two hours early.

Are you hungry or did you over eat? - It takes 4 hours to fully digest protein. Eat the very minimum of protein prior to a match, instead go with more high complex carbs with some healthy fats to give you all the energy you will need. I did not know how difficult I was making it on myself by eating large amounts of protein prior to a match, but it made me sluggish.

Are you in a focused mental state? - find some quiet time to visualize how you want to play that day. Get into a calm state. If you can allow yourself to get into the 'the zone' of highly concentrated on the ball only prior to the match you may get off to a very fast start. Prior to matches, I have my players say the following: "Today confidence is my biggest weapon. I will give 100% effort, enjoy the competition, show myself as strong and wise, and learn from my match. I get 65% of my first serves in play, my feet in position for every shot, and continually pressure my opponent, I love a tough match".

It is truly amazing how much more stable a players performances are from match to match after they get in the habit of repeating this mantra. The mantra contains four realistic match goals in regard to how to be on the tennis court, as well as stating confidence which has been proven again and again to be key to a good performance. Also, some physical objectives are in the statement which focus the mind on the how to win aspect without being too specific. Visualization has various aspects, one of which is making a statement that goes along with the picture of your perfect performance. Visualization can include having clear pictures of performing perfectly in your mind, making supporting statements about the same, and shadow swinging imagining the ball coming from the racket to the target area. Visualization can many times be the key that unlocks the potential for best performances, but can help increase the upper threshold of your absolute best.

On the other hand Steve Chandler says "Affirmations are like frosting on excrement", and he goes on to explain that all the affirmations and visualization in the world wont help you if you have not done any of the work of practicing your game! I would counter and say that visualization can help at any time, but coupled with great practice routines, then you will gain the most from the exercise.

Expectations

Have you ever had a match where you had very low expectations or someone you know had low expectations, and then played great?

Conversely, have you had high expectations that you would play nearly flawlessly and that your opponent was easily beatable, so you then played tight and did not play anywhere near your best? There is a delicate balance to be struck here. It's important to have some expectations. The mantra above give some clear expectencies, and creates a self commitment to do those things. When you focus on the mantra you are more likely to perform better, which of course increases your chances of coming out on top in the match. On the other hand if you have unrealistic expectations that you will win every match, and never make an error, or have many winners, aces or hit the lines, then you will be setting yourself up for disappointment. Focusing on the outcome of the match and raising your expectations can nearly prevent you from winning. However, focusing on the process of performing well and given the best possible performance in each point will not only give you a better chance of winning, but will help you to see that your performance may improve and you can satisfied with your play even in a loss.

Strategic - What is your game plan today? Do you know your opponent? Have 3 to 5 objectives on court to beat them. No more than 5 please... If you don't know your opponent, then imagine some different styles of opponents and how you adapt your game to exploit their weaknesses. Imagine yourself discovering their least favorite shot or two. Rehearse in your mind the first two shots, from your serve to their possible returns and how you will respond. Imagine hitting returns back to the server, deep crosscourt, low and wide, and sharply angled, and how you will move into position from each, also include some approach shots and winners on second serve return.

Visualize the Outcome - get a picture of playing great, another of competing hard for every point, another of showing strength, and finally shaking hands as the victor, thanking the person for the match. What ever you fear, imagine yourself conquering fear.

Talk with coaches or parents - Do you have a set routine for this? In my experience some talk can help you stay grounded, but too much talk can set your mind spinning, or have you feeling pressure. Set the parameters for what helps you achieve. Some players love to burn off some nervous energy by talking to EVERYONE. Even if that is so, you will want a period of time prior to your match to quiet yourself. I adopted a practice from the well know De La Salle football team. Their players practice only essential communication on game day. The whole culture of the school accepts that the players on Fridays will not talk much. Similarly, I have asked my high school teams to not socialize after school prior to a match, but to come straight to the courts, and as quietly as possible prepare for the days match. There will be plenty of time to talk afterward.

One Match Preparation

You may want to get a full 30 minutes of practice here. At least 10 minutes of groundstrokes, establishing rhythm, and dialing in your contact points is essential. If you know your opponent, have your practice partner mimic them for a moment. Many people like short court, and so do I, but only when done correctly. When you move your feet, and use precision footwork to get the precisely in the middle of your strings, then short court is a good thing. If its just a lazy exercise then that's a problem. In the remaining 20 minutes its advisable to hit at least 5 minutes of serves to get your shoulder fully warm, and 5 minutes of volleys. With the remaining ten minutes you could either serve or volley more, play some shot sequences, and/or play some points with your coach, parent or practice partner. I like 4 point sequences, so that you and your partner can have almost an equal amount of point play. If you play serve games and one wins at love and the other goes to deuce its not as fair to the practice partner. So play four points as server, and four as returner until you reach the 30 minutes.

Two Matches or More Preperation

Here you want to the things above, but want to conserve some energy. I like 5min,5min,5min,5min of each thing, but you know what you like. You might want to do 5,2,3,10 of Groundstrokes, Volleys, Serves and Point Play, or 10,2,5,3. Don't leave your energy on the practice court, but do raise your intensity at the end to full match play intensity so you will be ready for the beginning of your match. Mentally here, if you can begin to block out the notion of two matches, since really if you win the first one, THEN you have a second one. You must fully commit your energy to the first match to win it, and do so in the most efficient manner. I have seen players who did not give their all in the first match and lost, or prolonged it which sapped their energy for the second match which they then lost. If you have an opponent in your first match that you can easily beat, be sure to focus nicely on every point, making every attempt to come out of it 6-0,6-0 the tricky part is not to rush through this match. Also, as stated by Andrew Voss from Real Tennis Coaches "Use a resistance band, and/or a jump rope to get loose and get your heart rate up just prior to your match".

Visualize how to handle Second Serves

How well you hit your second serve, and how well you attack second serve are perhaps the most pivotal aspects of hard court play. Sometimes people don't think of a second serve for what it really is. Second serves are relatively weak shots that must be struck short in the court. The returner has a built in advantage, unless the server has a very well developed second serve. Even so, finding a way to attack a strong second serve is a huge indicator of your future success. When you successfully attack the second serve of the opponent and begin to win more than 50% of those points, you may even cause the player to take something off their first serve, to try for a higher percentage of first serves to protect themselves against having their second serve attacked. At that point, you may find you can return more first serves, while also attacking second serves. If you don't attack second serve, you will never realize this benefit. Another potential benefit of attacking second serves is that the player may feel so much pressure on second serves that they tighten up, or play to fine. They may double fault at key points in a match, because they know their second serve has to be deeper, faster or hit with more spin than they are accustomed. One of the all time true axioms of tennis is "you are only as good as your second serve". I would also add that you are only as good "as you attack second serves".

As the server, you want to develop great placement, and the ability to change placement accurately, then add spins and learn to vary to your spins, finally you will also need speed on your second serve to truly allow you to avoid attack. Varying spin and placement can really work to keep your opponent off balance.

One of the best pre-match goals is to attack the second serve of your opponent. You will be wise to learn all manners of attack. Obviously driving the ball with minimal topspin for a winner down the line is the most devastating to the server.

#

Realistic Match Goals

Jim Loehr wrote a piece on realistic match goals that I adapted somewhat and made my own. You would do well to study any book written by Jim. If you go into matches with realistic goals, and those goals are achievable and part of the process of winning then you will have your best chance of winning on the day if you achieve them.

1. **Give 100% effort.** It seems so obvious, but if you really look closely at it, 100% effort on every single point of a match is fairly elusive. Anyone can easily have a point where they give only 95% effort, not notice, then give 90% on the next point, and so on... until their intensity drops. Giving 110% effort is non-sense. How can you give 10% more than what you have? It's a bad strategy, because it leads to feelings of pressure, stress and over the top effort. People who say "I could have won" usually also say, "If I had given my best effort". These people protect themselves from finding out if they really were good enough to win.
2. **Enjoy the Competition.** If you are enjoying the sport, that's great, because its a game, and games are fun. If pair that with a will to win, then you really have something. I find that some people compete well, but have a hard time finding the enjoyment. Others truly enjoy playing, but don't mind losing, so then they lose more often than is necessary.

Share the joy of coming together to play a game of Tennis. Without the enjoyment, is it really that satisfying?

3. **Show yourself strong and wise.** Have strong body language, look the part of a confident fighter. Think the right thoughts. Have courage and stand up for yourself. Don't allow your opponent to cheat, manage the situation. Don't make excuses, have a clear mind in your match to see what is working and what is not. If execution is a problem, then execute better. A very powerful sequence of self talk is “I want to play better, I can play better, I will play better”.

4. **Learn from every situation.** Whether it’s a win, a loss or a practice. Take something away that was an improvement, and look for the lesson of the day to improve in the near future. Yes you can learn from a win, but many times a loss is a more fertile ground for learning. If you fail to learn from winning, then you lose an opportunity to put distance between yourself and the opposition.

Know Your Playing Environment

Tennis Courts

Hard Courts

Here in the U.S. there has been a strong trend toward slower playing hard courts with a higher bounce. When I was doing the most of my playing, it seemed there were an equal number of courts that would be called fast, medium fast, medium, slow or super slow. Nowadays there are few fast or medium fast courts, and and many more slow and super slow courts. This means the court grabs your shoes more, the spin of the ball has a different effect, because of the higher amount of friction point when the ball makes contact with the court.

Every day and every court plays a little differently. Know your court. A different court at the same site will have something different about it. People wrongly assume that a hard court is perfectly flat, and while some are flatter than others, many hard courts have cracks, bumps, undulations in the surface that can make the ball bounce this way or that.

At one high school where I coached, there was a crack diagonally set in the about 10 feet from the forehand corner on the right hand side. The court 'fell off' at that point, as the angle of the court was different by a few degrees. Our players understood that if you could hit that little drop off area, that you would hit a winner, and you could possibly cause the opponent to swing and miss. This created a strong home field advantage for our team.

There is a local indoor club that has courts set close together with divider netting between the courts. The netting is really too close to the doubles sideline. Most people who play at that court work on slice serves to make their opponent swing the racket to and through the netting. At first it's unnerving to feel your racket brush the netting, but after you get used to it, you can return those balls. Even so, its tough on visiting teams to play there at those courts.

I know of a few different hard courts that either have numerous raised bumps on the court, or undulations in the court surface that there is a strong unpredictable bounce of the ball.

Court Slant

Every hard court slants ever so slightly in one direction or one corner. Some courts slant heavily so that on one end of the court you might feel like you are six inches taller than the other player. Knowing how to play the slant of the court is a very large factor in success.

Here I will give you some general principles, then explain some certain courts that I know of and how those courts are unique. When you add a peculiar wind pattern for the location with the slant of the court, then you may find that a completely different style of play works best.

When the court slants uphill from one baseline to the other, then one player is on the uphill side and the other is on the downhill side. I know of numerous locations where this is the case as the court were constructed with a very aggressive slope for water drainage. When you are playing from the uphill side, your ball will travel out a bit easier, but will also bounce higher. Also, it will be easier to hit a winner, as your shot will be added in speed by the downhill roll of the ball. I recommend that you hit high deep topspin shots that can push your opponent back to the fence, wait for the short ball, then flatten out a shot for a down the line winner. From this side the net may seem lower, because you are a few feet higher, s o net clearance is not as much an issue as on the other side. Serving to the T on this side is encouraged for more than one reason, but mostly so that you make more serves, and keep your opponent from making angles. It's also easier to come to the net on this side, as it will be more difficult for your opponent to move forward for a passing shot, and also harder for your opponent to put you under much pressure with a defensive lob.

From the downhill side, it will be a bit more difficult to hold serve, so take even more care of your serves. The net will seem to be higher, so you do need to clear the net with your shots. The cool thing is that its easier to make your serve in, but harder to win the point outright. Because the court seems to rise up and 'accept' your shot, it will change the way you play a bit so that you don't play into the hands of the other player who wants to loop the ball way up. Since they are on the uphill side that gives them that advantage. Your advantage is that you can hit sliced, flat, angled serves and they will go in more often from the downhill side. Also, when hitting topspin groundstrokes you can make very good angles, and you should to keep your opponent moving. Additionally, flat and some slice groundstrokes early in a point can keep your opponent from looping the ball way up on you. If you exclusively hit high arching topspin from the lower side, you will be making it more difficult on yourself. Drop shots will be more effective from this side as well, because the ball will bounce back to you more readily, and not as much toward your opponent.

Courts that slant from Right to Left,

or Left to Right along the baseline.

Ask yourself, where is the court lower? Where is it higher? Where the court is higher, you can make a higher percentage of shots. Where its lower you can put your opponent under more pressure if you wait until you have moved into the court some to improve your percentages. One rule I use here is 'rally or angle to the high side, attack or approach to the low side". Defensive lobs to the high side, offensive lobs to the low side.

Courts that are high in the forehand corner one side, and lowest on the forehand corner of the other side. On these courts comparatively two of he opposite corners are relatively even in height, but one corner of the court is higher than the opposite corner. The same principles apply as above. Rally to the high side, attack to the relatively lower side. Playing from downhill to uphill as described above.

Courts that slant back from the net. From both sides the net seems higher. Definitely play as much topspin as you can. Work the point and as soon as you get a short ball make a great attack, as the downward slope on the other side will aid your attack. Be careful not to get too close to the net, because the slope on your side makes you more susceptible to the lob.

Courts that slant toward the net. This is rare, but I have seen two courts like this. Slice shots are premium. Hit big serves, use a lot of slice, come the net regularly, and get very close to the net. Even if you are lobbed the ball will practically bounce back to you. If one player plays a heavy topspin game against a slicing player, the slicing player has a huge advantage. On these courts you want to be at the net twice per game, hit a drop shot every other game, and mix up your serves between flat and slice serves.

Fast Courts, Medium, Slow,

and Uneven Courts

Depending on where you go, you will find a fairly wide variety of court surfaces. In the past faster courts were more prevalent, and nowadays slower courts are more prevalent. Also, there seems to be at least one brand of court surface paint material that creates an irregular bounce of the ball. As a result of informal research, it was confirmed that there are numerous players who experience this same effect at certain locations.

Fast Courts

An offensive game style with big serves, flatter shots, and net play will be rewarded! Also, playing some defense when your opponent is on the attack using shorter backswings can help you keep one more ball in play. Take charge of the point, don't wait around, it's first strike tennis. Players may slide and skid as they move.

Slow Courts

A grinding defensive style with a high percentage of first serves, heavy topspin shots and moving your opponent around is the main play on these courts. Be strong, but also patient, every shot should have a target, make your opponent be the first to give up a weaker shot, so you can attack. Only come to the net when you are sure that you have put your opponent way out of position. Traction and ability to make sharp turns on the court are helped by the slower surface.

Medium Courts

You may take a little time to discover how medium the courts are, and how you may play between a fast court style and a slow court style.

Uneven Courts

Some courts have a worn surface and you can see some smoother and more rough areas. Other courts have bumps, undulations, or cracks. Take a close look at those. Other courts may look to be very even but play uneven, you will know because the ball sometimes seems to be on you very quickly, and other times will seem to jump up and hang up in the air. These courts require that you be more patient with yourself as timing the ball may be difficult. When courts are painted the skill of the court painter and the surface paint selected have the largest bearing on the evenness of play. You may even see where there is more sand in one part of the court than the other, thus making that part of the court play more slowly than the other areas. Inspect the courts closely so you know where to expect bad bounces, low or high bounces. If there is an undulation on your opponents court, you might hit a certain shot there to take advantage of it. At one club where I worked there is a 'bird bath' in the forehand corner of the ad court. So any time you really need a point, then you can hit a kick serve into that area, and the bounce will many times go very high, impossible for the returner.

The Surface of the Court

In general the fastest courts are also the easier courts to move on, as you may be able to slide a bit in the court. The slowest courts may grab your shoe, and feel more difficult on your knees. It's a great idea to wear your newest pair of shoes for best traction on faster courts to avoid slipping. Conversely, keeping a pair of well worn shoes for a 'grabby' surface can help you move with more ease. At times I have advised my players to 'pick up their feet' as they run on a grabby surface and they do seem to move with more ease.

A spun tennis ball will behave differently on different speeds of surface. Faster courts don't accept the spin as readily. Accepting the spin means that the spin reacts the most to it's moment of friction with the court when the court accepts the spin. Generally faster courts don't accept the spin, so slice balls slide more, topspin shots don't jump up as much, and side spins wont immediately react off the court as fast. Aggressively sliced balls with stay very low! Kick serves will not be as effective, but slice and flat serves will.

The slowest courts accept spin the best. Topspin will jump, kick serves can get over shoulder or head height. Varying your spins can be very effective to create an less predictable ball for your opponent, as you can make the ball jump or die. Soft sliced shots can turn into almost no pace shots, that can force the opponent to create all the pace of the rally again. There is however one constant, if you can slice the ball with enough spin on your groundstroke and hit it with enough speed, you can get the ball so slide on a slower court, almost like skipping a rock on a lake. The deceptive bounce of that ball can be a real surprise to your opponent. One player well noted for playing ugly would hit varying kinds of slice and did a wonderful job of destroying the other players rhythm.

A final thought on hard court surfaces is that there is a general rule in regard to competition, that you do NOT want to wear a pair of shoes that you have just purchased and put them on just prior to playing a competitive match. This would be especially true if you have shoes with remarkable traction, and are about to play on a very slow court. Generally, shoes that might not have great traction on a faster surface generally work great on much slower surfaces, and vice versa. Unless you want to match your shoes to the surface, look for a middle of the road shoe in terms of traction. In my minds eye, I can think of one brand that is notorious for having players sliding around on the court, and another that seems to help players stop on a dime, so shop wisely and learn the sublets of how your shoes interact with the surface. That's one place where the rubber meets the road.

Clay Courts

Each clay court might as well have a different personality. Red Clay plays much slower than Green Clay, because its make from a softer material. Clay is not an area of expertise for me, but I do know that a lot depends on how much sun the court is exposed to at different times of the day, the outside temperature and humidity. Hot and dry conditions make for a faster court and will reward more aggressive tactics, and/or wrong footing your opponent. Damp or even wet conditions up to the point where the court is nearly unplayable, will slow the ball down so much, that a severe test of defensive will takes place. When a clay court plays at its fastest a considerable amount of net play is a great idea, and at its slowest, you would only want to come into the net when you absolutely must. The ball regularly takes a different sort of a bounce, and the court will play more nicely immediately after it has been dragged, but over the period of a few games when the ball creates pock marks on the court, each of those has the potential to create a ball that jumps up, left, right, or skips low.

Grass

Grass courts have a similar potential for odd bounces, but the courts generally are more slick. In wetter conditions the court very much rewards big first serves, and flatter shot making comparatively to hard courts.

Weather

Ideal conditions for a match seem to be about 65 to 80 degrees Fahrenheit. The ball won't react very unfavorably, and you wont have much trouble with dehydration from heat, or muscle tightness from the cold.

However above or below those temps, very dry or very humid climates, and wind in various forms can create opportunities for crises in how you play.

Wind Conditions Vary Widely

"It was windy" is not a very good analysis of how the conditions where. Just as Eskimos have 5,000 different words for snow, (or so I am told), so you should have many different understandings for types of wind and how it affects play on the day. Bill Tilden said flat out "It is almost impossible to slice or chop in a high wind". I would counter, by saying, on the day you can discover how successful you can be slicing into or with a wind, and how it might change on the other side of the court.

One thing you must always say is 'The wind is my friend' as your attitude about the wind has more to do with how well you play than it's actual effects on your game. One player who says,'The wind is my friend', has a considerable edge over the player who says 'I hate the wind'.

You can become even better friends with wind by understanding various types, and how it may affect play that day. Nearly constant wind in one general direction with minor variations in direction - the nice thing about fairly constant wind, is that it allows you to cope with it. You can toss a little bit in the other direction, allowing the wind to put your toss into the right location for you. No matter how it blows, you can adjust your game to take advantage of the benefits, and mitigate some of the disadvantages.

When you are facing a nearly constant wind from baseline to baseline, it will slow down, shorten and increase the effects of spin for one player, and speed up, lengthen and diminish the effects of spin for the other player. If you have a strong wind at your back, it will be easier to hit deeper in the court, whatever you do, you will most likely want shorter backswings. The wind in your face will make depth more difficult, but will make angles more dramatic, so set up an angle making game from that side of the court as much as possible.

If the wind is side to side alone the baseline, then shots that are a few feet in may be blown out, and a shots on the other side of the court may be blow in by that wind. Of course you need to adjust the targets in your mind, so that your shots will be blown in and not out. This can be more difficult than it sounds, so be patient as you figure out, just how far to hit the shot left or right so that will go where you want. I have played in a 40mph cross wind that seemed to blow the ball about 10 feet to the right on one side of the net and to the left on the other. I pledged never to play in that location ever again, because even though I love the wind, and tennis, those conditions simply were not very fun. On the day, I did manage to have a good attitude, and yet that wind was very extreme and the opponent played in that location often, taking advantage of the home field wind advantage. I bet you can tell that I did not win.

Wind that travels in one direction, but is on again and off again. You will need to be patient, and decide if you can wait a moment for the wind to stop while you serve. Also, you need to be constantly aware of a gust coming onto the court as it will suddenly take the ball with it. So you have to pay close attention, and be ready to make a last second move to the ball, if blown out of your ideal contact point.

Wind that changes direction and is on an off again. This makes life more difficult as you get a higher degree of unpredictability. This is one time that when you can, you want to 'hit through' the wind. So be sure ever time you can get set on balance that you hit a strong shot.

Swirling wind is the most difficult type of wind to play, as the ball is at its most unpredictable, it can go this way or that way. Many small circles of wind are blowing around the court, and they can suddenly change direction in the opposite way. It's a great idea to hit with a very minimum amount of spin, as the unpredictability of the ball along with the swing plans necessary for a good spin shot will create lots of mishit, misplaced shots. You may also find yourself off balance quite often. While of course you want to get into position as early as you can, be sure to delay getting your feet really set until the forward swing. Be sure also to be ready for a sudden change and work hard to get the ball in the middle of your strings. This type of wind is the great equalizer, so it comes down to the better player using superior movement training, and desire to win the match the priority over trying to look good and never losing a point. Some points will sure be lost because the wind made the shot nearly impossible. This will play equally on both sides.

When we understand something, like the wind, then it can be easier to accept it. Accepting a windy day in your mind can really strengthen you. Knowing the kind of wind and how it may affect play that day, is even more powerful.

Fog/Overcast/Humidity/Drizzle

When you play in these conditions the ball will retain some moisture, and the air is more dense with that moisture hanging in the air. The ball can feel heavier, and yet also like its harder to hit at the same speed as a sunny day. The advantage goes to the grinding style player on these 'heavy days'. On the other hand, a player with great touch can take advantage of the heavy conditions by play a light game. Sprinkling in drop shots, lobs, and various spins can be a great way to use the heaviness of the air for your purpose.

Note: the wild change in playing conditions from the Indian Wells professional tour stop, compared to Miami. Very rarely does a player do exceedingly well in both places, mainly because it's so dry and the ball flies in the desert of Indian Wells. In contrast, the Miami tournament must be among the most humid of the entire calendar. Flashier, more powerful, and creative players are rewarded in the dry air. Heavy topspin, strong physical players are rewarded in the heavy humidity.

Heat above 80 Degrees

The ball begins to fly off the Racket when it heats up. The player with more control of their shots will find that they now will have a little more power to be able to win some points outright. The powerful player could have a huge advantage because even more power has been added to the match, but it is all predicated on their ability to absorb some errors. Some power players go into a confidence melt down on warmer days, after they have made 2,3 or more errors in a row. The Power player needs to scale back their swing slightly, and/or add a bit more spin.

Heat above 95 Degrees

Pain really becomes a factor in the match, as many times your feet will burn when it's 95 degrees on court. If you have shade on your court, you definitely want to be in it for every possible moment. The same effect can occur and perhaps be heighten compared to 80 degrees. It can be a great idea to have another pair of socks, or even a fresh pair of shoes to put on after the first set. Be sure they are the same as the others. There is a story about a coach from Hawaii whose players sat under umbrellas on the changeovers. The players thought it made them look weak or dumb, etc. That team started to gain a huge advantage over the opposition on warm days. In a short while, most teams in Hawaii had umbrellas.

Heat well above 100 degrees

At some point over 100 degrees, it becomes harder to breath. Mentally this is a huge challenge, and you have to be able to do something mentally not to scream at every moment. I love very hot temperatures, or so I tell myself. Also, its very important to use good judgement. If you begin to show signs of heat stroke, or heat exhaustion, you can ask for a medical timeout and you should. At that time you should consider whether its wise to continue. I am not aware of all the consequences of continuing in a heat related illness situation, but I do know that you can create longer term issues for yourself. Do your own research, and don't try to be too tough. Back in the day, some players used to place a cabbage leaf in their hat, as a way to stay more cool. I tried it, it seemed to work very well.

Cramping - If you begin to cramp, then it's important to monitor that closely. My understanding of cramping is that you may have a small cramp say in a calf, a foot, or a hip. But if you are having a major muscle cramp in your thigh or gluteus, then it can be a sign of something much worse. I have witnessed seeing a player go from having a major muscle cramp into ***FULL BODY CRAMPING.*** That player had to be carried from the match, taken to the hospital for fluids. I was told by someone in the medical profession, (this is NOT medical advice), that the next stage is cardiac arrest. This should outline the serious nature of monitoring cramping. This definitely falls inside the category of living to fight another day.

Why is dealing with heat in a strategy book? First, because if you learn to avoid it, you have an advantage. Second, if you live to fight another day you can win more matches again more quickly. Third, being more fit over the longer term means you use less energy in victory and have more in the tank for a second match in a day.

I have heard umpteen number of remedies for cramping. Of course everyone's body chemistry is different, and you should seek the advice of a medical profession to discover the root causes. There is a particular product made from Calcium Ascorbate which I like a lot, and has worked for me and many of my player. Some players did not feel helped by it. I have heard 'drink this juice, drink that juice, have a sport drink, no not that one too much sugar' and all the info. Go check it out try it out and see what works. Calcium Ascorbate products generally work better when they have a full and balanced mineral complex. Also, the Vitamin C that you get aids in circulation, which is very important in avoiding cramps. I hear all the hype about sports drinks, but I still like cold water, and my Calcium Ascorbate because you can avoid sugar, and it also more closely matches the Ph of your blood.

Very generally speaking, but a dangerous thought is that in most cases cramping is caused by a lack of targeted conditioning. Something is missing from your conditioning program, or you are maybe doing too much of a certain training if you cramp often. The danger here, is that if you have some type of chemical imbalance, or other medical condition that is causing this, then ramping up your training is unwise.

Cool temps below 60 degrees

The ball will begin to behave differently at lower temperatures, it will be harder, and might feel heavier because of that. The weight of the ball does not truly change much, but the lower temperatures will make the court harder, strings have less elasticity, racquets less flex, and the ball is most affected. It can be a great idea to be sure to warm up your body longer prior to playing, especially because the above conditions will be harder on you. Also, stringing your racquets 2-5 pounds more loosely will help give you back some power, and remove some of the shock from the harder ball. Player a bit closer into the court to adjust to the reduced power is also a great idea.

Below 50 degrees

Tennis becomes much less enjoyable, and there is a dramatic difference in the bounce of the ball. Be sure to move forward at least a foot from your normal position.

32 degrees or less

The ball will barely bounce, and the use of deep / short combinations will be devastating. At some levels of the game, a well spun slice ball that stays low and skids can be unreachable.

At each level of lower heat, then you would need to prepare your body even longer. I once attempted to teach a lesson in 25 degree weather, and the balls did not bounce sufficiently for any value to come from it. Additionally, I played a match in 31 degree weather, that allowed me to outsmart my opponent, with many low slow shots. When I returned to the even the next day some people asked me if I was just visiting, I said "No, I'm here to play. I won yesterday". There was shock and disbelief because truly the other guy was a much more highly noted player than me. I beat him fairly easily, as he did not warm up as well as I did, and he never adjusted to my strategy, consistently popping up balls at the net that I could volley away easily.

When it's very cold, a softly hit ball with very little spin, about one foot over the net, can have a second bounce that is just a few feet beyond the service line on the down the line. If the player is standing at the baseline or behind, then they will find it difficult to hit any technically sound shots from that point of the court. This same shot can be affective in almost any conditions, but is works best when everything in the environment is slow.

To conclude this section, playing in conditions can have a subtle to a very significant impact on how you play the game. In fact, a winning game on the day in the conditions may not resemble anything in your Plan A, Plan B, because you are clearly going to have to use plan C, D, or Z. On the other hand there may be a subtle change in how the ball flies, and you can use that to your advantage, or the other player can, so be aware of it.

A great question to ask yourself is, "Am I stuck on the style and game plan I use, or would I rather win the match?"

Please get unstuck. Learning to win in crazy conditions can lead to the most memorable stories of your career. One day I played a two hour and a three hour match in temperatures that started at 100 degrees at the beginning of the match, and ending with 107 degrees. So learn to win in all conditions, and know which adjustments will help you on the day.

#

Pace of Play

The returner by rule plays to the pace of the server. In good conscience, for sportsmanship, you will need to prepare yourself as fast or slow as the server does so within the 20 seconds. Within the rules there are some things you can do to affect the pace of play. As the server, you really have control to play almost as fast as you want. Your comparative fitness level with your opponent, along with your stress and tension levels will dictate how quickly you might want to play. There is some science to this, but mostly there is an art to playing at or changing the pace of play.

The Science of Pace

It has been shown in a study that servers are more accurate when they allow their heart rate to recover to a lower level prior to serving. Conversely, returners had better reactions and quickness while having a slightly elevated heart rate. Additionally, many experts agree that a 3:1 rest:work ratio is ideal for Tennis. So if you played a 60 second or longer point, then you will most likely want to use the entire 20 seconds prior to playing the next point. Early in a match you might not feel the need for as much recovery, even so if you are the less fit athlete on the day, you may want to use it anyway. As the match wears on, then full use of the recovery time between points can be essential to victory.

When you are the fitter player, and can play at a faster pace and coax that from your opponent, then the advantage is yours. When serving, be sure your heart rate comes down some, get the balls, plan the point and serve. As the returner you can return to the line more quickly and show readiness, which can work to make the server feel as though they must serve right away. As the server, don't fall for this trick. All of this is within the rules.

The Art of Pace

Jim Loehr has a famous intervention for players called the 16 second cure, and as you can see from the name, you might have to practice it to get it to fit within the 20 seconds. Loehr speaks of the mental closure at the end of the point, then a moment of relaxation, followed by mental preparation for the next point in terms of intensity and strategy, then a ritual that provides something predictable to the match for you. Early in a match you may not need to use all four elements, but during a difficult, nervous, or fatigued part of a match you may want to do all four elements. See Jim's books for much more information on this.

Between points sometimes your opponent may have the behaviors that are annoying to you either intentional or not, you can find something else to pay attention to, so that are you drawn into the negativity of the annoyance.

Ultimately, its your ability to let down and have a moment of a rested mind and relaxed body that will help you as a match wears continues. I find that most players under 4.5 are not as aware that they have an increasing amount of stress in their mind and body.

A general axiom that may work for you is "when leading play faster, when behind play more slowly". Playing faster without rushing can help you to close the match more quickly. Playing a bit more slowly may give you the right amount of think time to discover the way to win the match.

An interesting exercise that can help you learn to be a front runner playing fast, or be the player who lengthens a match to find a way to win is called "The Egg Timer Set". I take two players, one whom I think will win 6-0 over the other, and I put them on court. I give the favorite 20 minutes to win the set. There is no expectation as to score. I tell them: "Be sure to play quickly without rushing, and concentrate on winning every point. Every point you lose costs you some time". I take the opponent aside and say "I don't know if you can win the match, but you can play for 20 minutes or longer. Take your time, work as hard as you can to win every point you possibly can. Maybe the favorite will get bored or frustrated". Later, I may take more closely matched opponents and use a 30 or 35 minute limit. Which ever player succeeds, then the next time the time limit changes by 2 or 3 minutes to make it even more challenging. Since the average set takes 37 minutes, then anything over that time does not really create any additional challenge.

The Rules

Between points there are 20 seconds from the time of the end of the last point, until the serve must start the next point. There is no time limit between first and second serve that I know. This has changed in the past, so be sure to keep up with the latest rules. There are 60 seconds from the completion of one game until the start of the next. Also, after the first game there is no break, simply a change of sides. After the third game you may use 90 seconds.

If you are playing someone who is gaining an advantage by breaking these rules, you are best advised to caution them to play a little faster. If this were to continue be sure to get an official to monitor the times between points, games, or on changeovers. Some famous players have broken these rules and smart opponents have made issue of it, in order to help them play to a pace that is within the rules. Why would you want to play someone who is a very good player and then also allow them to break the rules?

Of course, its wise to be graceful in situations where someone is ill, hurt, a ball goes over the fence, or there is some other distraction.

Post Match

Cool Down

Especially in a situation where you have two matches in short order, one after the other, the cool down is vital to great recovery, and then preparation for the next match. A great cool down will have an impact on how sore you might be the next day from a tough match.

Post match reflection: After you have had a few minutes to relax , cool off relax and get something to eat, its good to reflect on your match and take a few notes. Go through your strokes, how did you serve today, volley, groundstrokes, where their specialty shots that were excelled or cowld have been better? Visualize immediately the improvement you need.

Coaching Post Match

Anyone coaching a player, the post match critique is something that needs to be negotiated. You need to know your player and how they respond to winning or losing. Also, whether or not they won or lost, how do they respond to a great or poor performance or something in the middle. Generally, its a good idea to give the player some space after a win. Let them soak in their accomplishment. Some players will want congratulations. After a loss, it may be a great idea to show some token of support, whether its coming nearby, a brief and appropriate hug, or maybe a show of support by saying something nice to them. You have to be careful, as you want to show support, but this would not be the time to criticize. "Let me know when you are ready to talk about it" is a good thing to say. It's generally true that losses are where the most learning comes from in a players career. There are exceptions, so you have to be careful. In football, there are games where the coaches will delete the game film, because the performance was so poor, they don't want the team to see it. There are times when you just have to completely forget about an awful day on court, and move forward. Reviewing every ugly detail is not going to help the player to move forward with confidence. Fortunately, as players move along they will have less frequent truly bad performances. When I was a kid any significant loss might mean a full week of sulking. Even as an adult, I was not ready to hear any constructive criticism until at least 24 hours after a loss. There seems to be a sliding scale for how soon the player will receive coaching, based on how competitive they are. I have been hyper competitive in my life for the most part.

Player 'System' Entry Points

In the system of how a player engages the ball, there are different entry points into that system to begin to effect change on how a players play.

1. Friction of feet on the ground.

2. How solid is your contact point

3. Knowing the path of: a. the incoming shot and b. the plan for the outgoing shot.

4. The swing path that has the strings addressing the ball with the intended ideal location, angle, speed, and body rotation.

A player may approach their game from any of these systemic entry points, but I recommend that everyone try first to connect with the feet. If you begin and end your game on balance, then many of the other objectives become so much easier. One thing quite common among the very best players in the world, is that their movement is so precise that they find themselves on balance for a 'still moment' prior to most every shot. Getting or keeping your opponent off balance or never set for their shot is a key element in winning a match. Lesser players do not move quite as well and will more frequently be off balance which affects the quality of the shot, then provides greater opportunity to their opponent. When I ask my players what the goal of footwork is, they quite often say "To get to the ball", but that is not a complete understanding of what you are trying to achieve. The goal of footwork is to get in position with the ball in the center of the strings, in the best possible balanced position so that you experience a still moment just prior to your forward swing. Hitting the cleanest possible ball strike on every shot is quite a strategy. Generally, the player who hits the ball more cleanly has a huge edge in the match.

Everything is connected. The first step can't be quick without the eyes detecting the ball coming from the opponents strings. However, the response of a split step, or bounce hop to initiate movement is paramount. Best practice seems to be to learn ever possible footwork step, movement, rotation, because the game is now played in 360 degrees of movement. Anyone who takes a stylistic, or simplistic approach to this is missing out on the full variety of movement. Anyone who takes an system analyst approach, is missing out on the trained automatic instinctual movement that players need. YOU CANT BE THINKING ABOUT YOUR FEET WHILE YOU PLAY. If you are thinking about your feet, your awareness of the ball will be diminished. The great Tom Stow encouraged his players to take up dance, and any other form of movement study, not as an analysis, but as a way to give complete freedom. There are comprehensive footwork studies to be found. Get them. Practice them with no pressure of making a shot. Move every way possible. Arrive on balance. Nothing else matters. Recently, Scott McCain spoke, and he is a coach on the ATP tour, describing the new movement and how more and more you see a 'bounce', 'float', 'land'. The first move many times will be a bouncing hop, and might include a body turn, then the players adjusting steps will appear as though they are floating across the ground, as they have rebounded from their previous bounce hop, and finally, just before contact, one or both feet will really land on the court. Truly engaging one or both feet with the ground allows the player to develop greater ground reaction force which is a huge key to developing more power in your game. So once you have reacted to the ground, now all that energy will travel through the kinetic chain and arrive finally at your contact point.

Contact points are also affected by the eyes, but the hand comes in at this time. Of course the hand has a grip on the handle, and the effectiveness of this grip at this contact point comes into question. Here is whether you decide if its ok to change your grip, how often and in what way. If you do not ever change your grip you fall prey to the weakness inherent in your gripping style. Everyone needs to be able to have a Semi-Western and a Continental Grip and maybe someone in between. Playing only Full

Western will limit you. These days, Eastern Grips seem to require that the player be a minimum of 6'2" and maybe much taller to handle the higher contact points in today's game. Top players quickly identify the player who only uses a western grip and they find moments to use a slice shot, knowing full well the high percentage of short balls they will receive immediately following that sliced shot will allow them to attack in any variety of ways.

#

The Debate Between Power and Control

There might not be one way to develop a championship tennis player. I have heard some coaches say that control of the shot is everything, and that power will come much later. Of course there are quite a few well noted coaches who start with power, making that the building block of a players game, then working to control it. Still others might say a full compliment of shot making ability. It's really up to the player to decide, while of course listening to an expert coach. We all have different capacities for power. Here is a brief story of how one player was more naturally aggressive and the other had worked to learn it: It was a match between a player who had made a splash early in their career and had always been blessed with great power and no fear of playing aggressively, against the later maturing player who had more slowly worked her way up to the top 10 in the world. This was a number of years ago. The higher ranked player who had shown better results over her career including grand slam wins had been trained with power from the beginning. The challenging player on the day had always been consistent, but was building more and more power and risk taking into her game. A tremendous power battle ensued. It was a tremendous match as both players powered the ball ruthlessly, and the smarter player seemed to have the edge. Each player winning a close set. At 3-all in the third set, the player who had lately become more powerful shrunk back slightly from the attacking groundstroke mentality, and the player who had been playing powerfully, practically from birth, won the match 6-3 in the third in the space of a few minutes time. In a crisis situation, people respond in their best level of training. The one player had been trained to be powerful her entire life, and the other less than 18 months, and it showed on this day. So as you begin your training, know where you want to finish, so that you can have years of training so that your game really becomes who you are, then you will find you can play it bravely to the end.

Take another player, well noted for being extremely consistent, winning many clay court events, with some fair results on very slow hard courts. He had not been passed the quarterfinals of a hard court event in the early years of his career, and seemed to do very poorly when the courts were faster. He then doggedly began to work on developing more power on his shots by reducing the amount of topspin, to go along with his great defensive style. In less than two years he became #1 in the world. But first, he needed to learn to hit his shots through the court, rather than only hitting heavy topspin on every shot. That player? Rafael Nadal, who also then worked hard on his volley game to give him a better chance at Wimbledon.

Two other players I know of who where solid top 10 performers were known for either power, or great consistency, but when they learned to sporadically attack the net to show a change of pace and finish points more quickly, then they became #1 in the world. Jim Courier and Mats Wilander.

Chris Evert, the greatest model of consistency in the history of the women's game had to make a dramatic change to her style of play, as Martina Navritilova began to dominate the WTA Tour, with not only had a powerful serve, but also a wide variety of spin shots to go with legendary volleys. Chris by becoming much stronger, improved in power, and also added more net attack to her game to regain the #1 ranking.

There are problems to be found and solved in working to become a better and different player. The payoffs are great when you make a commitment to a change in the character of your game. It requires a commitment to becoming a new player. I believe in your decision about how you want to set out to play. If you are more of a perfectionistic person, and many errors will make you crazy, then set out to play as error free as possible. Even so, you will need to make take some calculated risks in order to excel. If you are more artistic or open, then play a powerful or artistic game, but learn to cut down on errors little by little. It is important to remember that there can be some major mistakes made in this regard. One notable player had worked his way into the top 10 in the world, with an all out net attacking game, then with advice of a coach he began to work on his ground stroking game more so that he could have longer rallies. His ranking dropped very quickly as he went so fully away from the unique style that made him such a tough match up. So, you need to make a balanced decision about how far to take these changes. As a young player, ultimately, no one is going to want to play you if you get mad at every error, or if you make so few shots in the court that they can't even keep a rally going. Once you get started, talk to your coach to collaborate on how to get from where you are to where you want to be.

I have a very collaborative adult player that I have coached for almost two years now, and he is 6-1 and over 200 pounds. Very solidly built. He told me that he wants to be more consistent. I agreed that making fewer errors is a good idea, but I don't like the word 'consistent' as people use it to beat themselves up. Very few people are very happy with their 'consistency' when they finish a match. Also, a more aggressive style will suit his physique so much better than trying to be someone who maintains long rallies to wear down the opponent. He bought into the idea that because of his size, he wont often be the quicker player on the court, but he can be the more powerful player, and his game should center around power. 2,3,4 shot rallies are going to be what suit him best. Big serve, Big Forehand, win or lose the point. Long rallies will not go in his favor very often.

The bottom line here is to have a long term plan for becoming the player you want to be, and to be as complete a player as you can be, while managing your confidence, knowing YOUR game prior to the most important events.

#

Story of Discovery

The #1 player at a high school, who also had a good USTA Sectional ranking, had a nice amount of variety to his game to go with a good amount of power, although he wasn't the fastest player on court. It was imperative for him to start a point well, gain control and stay in control of a point. Playing a rival school, who had a player who was nearly his equal, my player was playing even, or might have been down a break. I noticed something in the match. If my player sliced to the two handed backhand of the opponent, the reply shot would be another slice that would float and land short. So, we used that information and whenever he really needed a point, then he would slice low to the backhand, get a weaker ball and attack it in different ways. My player came from behind to win in straight sets.

It only seemed natural and smart to go into the next match ready to use a steady stream of low slice shots, so that was the game plan. Just one problem, the opponent had understood how they failed in the previous match and obviously solved the problem. So when my player hit the low slice, the opponent countered with a heavy topspin angled ball to my players backhand side and short, landing near the service line, which put my player out of position. My error as coach was to encourage my player to try to slice better and see if he could end that shot. It never worked. In fact, as soon as my player attempted to anticipate the sharp angle cross court shot, the opponent would poke the ball down the line for a winner. My player lost that day. The next day I told my team "I am glad we won as a team, but our #1 match, I take responsibility, because I came up with a game plan that did not work. Give credit to the opponent for being a smart player. Also, I appreciate our #1 player for trusting me and working hard to make the game plan work. It turns out we could have been more flexible with the game plan, which I was not. It won't happen again". In the final meeting my player used the slice only sparingly, and we had developed a different game plan and he won in straight sets in dominating fashion for a league title.

How to End Cheating in Junior Tennis: 21 Ways to Eat an Elephant

The Elephant in the Front Room

"There'a a phrase, "The elephant in the living room", which purports to describe what it's like to live with a drug addict, an alcoholic, an abuser. People outside such relationships will sometimes ask, "How could you let such a business go on for so many years? Didn't you see the elephant in the living room?" And it's so hard for anyone living in a more normal situation to understand the answer that comes closest to the truth; "I'm sorry, but it was there when I moved in. I didn't know it was an elephant; I thought it was part of the furniture." There comes an aha-moment for some folks - the lucky ones - when they suddenly recognize the difference." – Stephen King

Our tennis family is in trouble. We need therapy. There is an elephant in the room that has long been ignored. Some pretend that the elephant is not a problem or that they really don't mind elephants, while others say that having an elephant in the room develops character. Life has prepared me to deal with the elephant. I never would have considered that growing up in this dysfunctional family known as tennis would turn into a strength, but it has. Now, let's name the elephant: The elephant in the room of junior tennis is cheating. It comes in many forms from outright lying, to gamesmanship and even intimidation. At a recent Tennis Summit, there was a seminal moment when the the panel discussion led by Kurt Kamperman of the USTA, including Dan Santorum (PTR), John Embree (USPTA) and Paul Lubbers (USTA), all agreed that cheating in juniors has reached epidemic proportions. They also agreed that it is a key factor in causing players to leave the sport. This is an elephant-sized problem.

It's easy to be overwhelmed by the size of the problem, but if we think outside the box and tackle the problem slowly and methodically we can solve it. Perhaps you have heard this old joke: How do you eat an elephant? The answer is one bite at a time. This is our situation. One person eating alone will not reduce the size of anything very quickly. So let's assume that thousands of tennis stakeholders are reading this and will participate in solving this problem. There is courage in numbers and together we can reduce the size of the problem one bite at a time.

We need to understand what a complex problem this is. We can't take a scorched earth approach in dealing with it. I have run many tournaments of my own and those sanctioned by various organizations. Over the course of my 27-year career I have observed that about 80% of the "bad calls" are due to one simple fact: Making calls is a difficult task. I believe that 15% of actual bad calls come as a result of a player wanting to win so badly that they become psychologically blinded, and they sincerely believe or want to believe their opponent's ball is out. Let me add here that having that trait is a key indicator of a passion and drive in the child. It is of course unethical to make a bad call out of your passions but it at least shows moxie. Finally, I'd like to call the last 5% "criminally bad calls". These are the calls that make us want to jump on the court and right the injustice. These are the calls where it's break point and the ball is clearly on the line, but the opponent can't deal with the loss. So, in order to "speed things along for me" and win a little easier and save some energy, the ball is out. Perhaps we too have even been guilty of the 5%. We reason it away because "all the other kids are doing it." Some contend that, at a national level, the percentage of criminally bad calls calls is much higher, but no one really knows. Why? Because the problem has been ignored for far too long. What a shame for a player to spend so much money on plane flights, hotels, rental cars, eating out and more only to face a high likelihood that they will be cheated, and may be tempted to lower themselves to the same level of their cheating opponent. Much of the thinking about how, when and why to cheat plays out subconsciously in the player, but unfortunately, in the minds of some it is a conscious deliberate decision.

Players make mistakes. There is an intense internal pressure to win. Sometimes the pressures are external and a child is dealing with extreme or even abusive pressure from parents or coaches. It is good to keep this in mind because the factors leading to the child's decision to cheat are important and inform how we help that player. Let's make the case here that all players can be helped and coached to play by the rules no matter how bad their cheating may be.

The sad thing here is that there are systematic problems in our sport. There are so-called 'tennis academies', which should be growing the child as much as they are growing the tennis player, but these academies have a high percentage of players who make bad calls. Some of these academies actually teach parents how to send signals from the sideline, and use different forms of gamesmanship, such as trying to confuse the score, to intimidate and annoy the opponent. 'Academy' suggests an educational component, but no such character building is taking place. It doesn't reflect well on the academy for the child to lose. These are not tennis academies they are businesses. Beware of them. If all the good people who want the sport bettered bring enough pressure to bear, even those academies will need to change their way of doing "business".

#

The Cat, the Tree and the Snake

"And so these men of Indostan
Disputed loud and long,
Each in his own opinion
Exceeding stiff and strong,
Though each was partly in the right,
And all were in the wrong!" -John Godfrey Saxe (1816-1887)

Three blind men approached an elephant (sorry, one more elephant story). One touched its tale and said, "It's a cat." Another felt the rough skin of its big round leg and said, "It's a tree.", and the other ran their hands along the trunk and exclaimed, "It's a snake." The lesson here is that it's very easy to see a problem through the lens of our own experience. We all learn in life that we are supposed to view problems objectively. The bird's eye view helps us tackle the problems on the ground.

What we can't do is scapegoat, blaming others for problems we ourselves can fix. The coaches may say, "It's the sanctioning body, or the parents' fault". The parents may say, "It's the other parents, coaches or sanctioning body's fault", and, you guessed it, the sanctioning body may blame themselves and the other two. In order to solve the problem we need to stop fixing the blame.

In a recent conversation with Bill Mountford, we agreed that not all solutions are practical for every situation. However, I am confident that at least one, if not two or three of the following action items, can be implemented by everyone. Take a look at the list below. I want to challenge you to commit to two or three of them for the remainder of the year. Then, next year, take on additional items that may be out of your comfort zone. Commit now!

Take this pledge: "I (your name) pledge to help reduce the problem of cheating along with the other thousands of stakeholders using two or three of the following strategies."

The first tenet: Play by the rules! We have all felt the following angst: How can I enjoy the game when I know there is the real possibility that the other player can cheat and use gamesmanship without consequence? A fair competitive environment in any game or sport obviously requires the establishment of rules, but more than that, it requires the observance of those rules. In an ideal world, players who do not follow the rules are penalized, but we don't live in an ideal world. The policing of those rules is of grave concern to the competitors and those who are guardians of the game. Protecting the rules protects the good people who follow them. Their governance should be one of the main jobs of the sanctioning body of any tournament. Without fair play, there can be no game.

At the same Tennis Summit mentioned earlier, a panel discussion addressed the best practices in coach and player development. Everyone on the panel wholeheartedly agreed that sportsmanship and character development, especially in our junior players, is of vital importance if our game is to thrive. Additionally, each affirmed that in recent years, greater emphasis has been placed on educating coaches and tennis professionals in this area. Currently, though, it was stated that 38% of junior tennis players who play one tournament quit playing tournaments after that first experience. In addition, very few players get to as many as six tournaments, a watershed mark if they are to continue to play the game. Much of the health of our sport relies on large-scale participation in sanctioned competitive play. How can we make tournament play fun and enjoyable? The answer is clear: By building young men and women who care as much about honor, integrity, and commitment as they do the line call they are tasked to call. If we commit to this, we will arm coaches, parents and players with a positive action step to help young players compete beyond a few tournaments.

~~~~~~~

It is not an exaggeration to say that one horrible experience with an opponent who engages in gamesmanship can be devastate a young tennis player, turning them away from sanctioned competition forever. Others due to a multitude of negative experiences walk away from the sport asking, "Do I really want to continue in a sport that allows open and willful cheating?"

The lack of oversight with regard to gamesmanship, if truth be told, causes otherwise honest coaches and parents to teach a fight-fire-with-fire approach, telling their young players that if you determine an opponent is cheating outright and continuously then you have the right to level the playing field by calling their balls out. To beat the monster you have to be the monster. Recently I interviewed a high-level junior who is a budding
~~~~~~~

pro-level player and she estimated that at the national level junior events, 15% of players in the draw are known cheaters. I believe that she was being kind by underestimating the problem slightly. If she is correct, that means that at least one in seven players cheats at that level. I think we can agree that a percentage that high is staggering.

If you ordered dinner at a nice restaurant and your food came back cold, or wasn't prepared to your specifications, you would send it back without much thought. Of course, you may try to be as polite as possible so as not to offend the server and chef, but it's not what you ordered. In the same way, if you are the consumer of a tennis tournament, and the match you are served is not played according to the rules, you would want to send it back. When the match is played in conditions that are clearly unfair, and the spirit of competition is violated, the player must take action. If a player believes they can steal the match by making bad calls and use gamesmanship to tilt the overall advantage their way, then it's best to take polite but firm action. Parents and players can politely gain the attention of a tournament official to alert them to the problem. Most all of us have done this only to have the official then leave after a few games as though their mere presence had solved the problem. If the behavior continues the proactive player should firmly and respectfully ask the linesperson to stay for a longer period of time. In my mind, it's far better for an official to stay parked on a court where there is a known problem than it is for them to unobtrusively linger around the fences of many matches having no real effect on play.

As a coach, I have seen my own players, to whom I teach sportsmanship, fall prey to players who have been taught to cheat and disrupt. Those players make bad calls, confuse the score, place their towel on the court to distract, whine and shout regularly, preen and posture, fail to return the ball on one bounce, or fire it back fast in order to intimidate. These coaches and parents have no consideration for the dignity of the player. All the while, slowly and methodically, these adults are teaching these kids a disregard for honor, integrity, and commitment to something bigger than themselves. If this were not enough, when otherwise good kids with strong morals are encouraged to fight fire with fire as their only defense against cheating, then the system poisons them as well. What are we to do?

#

The Power of Community

"Never underestimate the power of a small group of committed people to change the world. In fact, it is the only thing that ever has."
Margaret Mead

I know what you are thinking: you are think that I am going to call on you to be a watchdog, to police the cheaters. I am not going to do that. Rather, I am going to ask you to influence through numbers. There are other parents who have experienced the same frustrations. They are all around you at every tournament. Go to them. Talk with them about the issues, but please stay away from placing a scarlet "C" on the worst cheaters. Don't let the conversation become a name calling session. You will fail in your mission if it goes in that direction. The objective going forward in this community approach is to win people to a cause. This involves compassion and understanding for every child playing.

Yes. the worst offenders must be dealt with. A tournament is like a large classroom, and a wise teacher will first deal with the worst behaviors that disrupt the classroom, and only then begin to work on the other behaviors. Fixing the worst cases quickly transforms the classroom into a peaceful and engaging place for learning. This is the approach that eventually must be taken, but we need to do it together and with caring purpose. Together we can take positive steps to remedy gamesmanship.

There is a movement starting in Florida tennis called The PAC (Players Against Cheating). They have a website and Facebook page you can join (www.playersagainstcheating.com and facebook/playersagainstcheating). The idea in this movement is to bring the kids together in local chapters in order to create positive peer pressure amongst themselves. The movement is run by and for the kids, no adults or coaches allowed. Parents are encouraged to organize bowling parties or other outings with the members to create cohesion and respect for one another, but that is the sole role of the parent and coach. Hopefully the movement will gain ground and become a force for good in our tennis community.

#

Solutions for Everyone

"Trust is the glue of life. It's the most essential ingredient in effective communication. It's the foundational principle that holds all relationships." Steven Covey

1. **Celebrate Sportsmanship** - Whether your player wins or loses, if they played with good sportsmanship, let them know. The same goes for the opponent. I like to say: "Nice match, I enjoyed watching two good sports play today". Not all young people will admit it, but they do love praise and they take notice. It is basic to our human nature to be supported and appreciated for our efforts and it is a strong motivator. This is why minor indiscretions should be overlooked and the celebration of a match played in a spirit of good sportsmanship should be recognized. Likewise, our first comments should not always address the skill of the player; rather, when great sportsmanship is in play, we should take that opportunity to express appreciation. Our comments over time will make a difference.

2. **Pick Your Battles** - Not every act of poor sportsmanship needs to be addressed immediately. You can be fairly certain that if you have very strong feelings about what you are witnessing on the court, there are others who have potentially the same strong feelings who are seeing it opposite of the way you are seeing it. War is possible at these times so realize that that moment is probably not the best time to engage. Carefully consider that the only thing people remember is your anger, and not facts surrounding the point in question. It is best for you and your player to be the cool-headed influence and look for the right time to address the issue.

This is especially hard when the issue is not a single infraction but a cascade of events: I once had a situation as a tournament director where I watched a player bemoan most every point won by his opponent, question the competency of his opponent, and use every trick to annoy him. In between points, he rarely returned balls to the other player on one bounce. He would hit them in the far corner or drop them short. He placed a towel on the court as a distraction. The antics came to a head when he threw his racquet about as hard as I had ever seen a racquet thrown and I immediately defaulted him. Of course this was dangerous and someone could be hurt. This was clearly behavior to be penalized. Reflecting back, I wondered why the victim never stepped up and brought it to the attention of the officials. I was, after all, right there. When you witness something this egregious, it has to be stopped. Drive a stake into the ground and confront this issue until it is resolved, before racquets are thrown and someone gets hurt.

#

3. **Step by Step** - Pick ONE major battle to fight per year. If you witness a match that involves cheating or gamesmanship, follow up on that match with the tournament director and sanctioning body, and do so in a professional manner with a clear, concise letter devoid of any personal attacks. If what you witness has you feeling angry, that is a good sign that it's worth a fight. However, let all of your feelings subside prior to writing the letter. I have had people write legitimate complaint letters regarding my own tournaments, but few of them were ever written in a professional and concise manner. Constructive feedback is important. It actually does make tournaments better. Officials want your participation as long as your actions move the ball forward. When I receive a respectful and professional letter that focuses only on a few manageable items, it helps me do a better job. Conversely, if I receive an angry letter that contains a laundry list of items that nit-pick factors outside of our control, then it diminishes my motivation to respond. So consider your words and the focus of the written response. Those reading the letter may look past the content of the argument if they sense hostility in the tone of the writing. Sanctioning bodies also tend to discount what is being said when voiced in anger. Do this once per year, and you will see a change.

#

4. **Don't Demonize, Empathize** – Ask yourself this question: What is driving this kid to make bad calls? Do they face significant pressure at home to win? Is their vision 20/20? Is their coach a maniac driving the kid too hard? How bad do they want it? Consider that there may be other factors under the surface that can be addressed and then, with this in mind, go to the official. Your conversation might then go something like this: "Sir, I'm not sure what is motivating the player on court #5 to make balls calls but he has done so now more than 5 times." This will actually place the official in the position of authority and make you, in his eyes, a caring individual interested in fair play.

Your empathy can even include the desire to see the other player grow in their understanding of the importance of fair play. A linesperson can help them come to grips with their calls. In the presence of an official, one that is on court, I have rarely seen players continue their behavior. It is difficult to rationalize away a good ball when an official challenges your call. The player might think to themselves, "That's your opinion," but they will rarely give voice to those thoughts and challenge the linesperson. This is good training for the cheater. Acts of honesty require training. There are countless kids who were never taught the importance of ethical behavior. Their parents are likely adrift also in that department. Objective third parties, in moments like these, are welcome.

Recently, one of my players asked for a linesperson in a match where many bad calls were made. She actually lost the first set because of the calls. Late in the second set, the linesperson finally arrived, and they split sets. On the first point of the third set tie-breaker, my player hit a ball on the line, the opponent called the ball out. My player then challenged the call and the linesperson overruled the call. At this point I was beginning to think that this girl had been trained to see those balls as ‘out’. Anyway, she was clearly upset. After a few more points she made another bad call. She was overturned again. The girl seemed genuinely distraught at the overrules. That was all I needed to see. She simply saw it differently. Her training, I concluded, on what constituted an out ball was flawed. The reversal of two calls in the tie-breaker preserved the match for my girl who went on the next day to win her very first tournament. If the official had not been there, my player would likely have lost and been robbed of her first tournament win. My hope in that moment was for the other girl. My hope was she learn and grow. I expect to see her again making better calls.

#

5. **Support Well Run Tournaments** - Promote events that take sportsmanship seriously. Lisa Stone of Parentingaces.com has begun to publish her tournament director of the year award, and it’s a lovely list as voted on by the 25,000 followers of her blog. If your child’s goal is to move onto national level tournaments, I would highly recommend that you follow her blog, as she covers the national scene providing a place for comments and ideas. Once you find the great events, praise and promote them to your friends. Tournaments that are committed to fair play are often not attended by cheaters. If they do attend, they tone it down and clean up their calls. Commit to those events and tell your friends. Conversely, avoid the poorly-run events.

A friend told me the following story about an experience at an event:

“My family had made a habit of traveling to a particular national junior tournament (a tournament for 12 and under juniors only) and on every occasion, we had experienced rude parents and cheating children. The leaders of the event would confront the wrongdoers, but they never removed anyone from the event, regardless of the offense. On our last attendance, the mother of the other child addressed my 8 year old, demanding that he call a ball out or in and not sit there in his uncertainty. She wasn’t careful and caring about it either. She was told to restrain herself from addressing my son. Later, the father, after another questionable line call (remember this is a couple of 8 year olds), walked down the fence line to my sons side of the court and as he walked by mouthed, “little punk.”

I bristled. But, as luck would have it, the head tournament official was standing right there. She addressed this father in no uncertain terms and made him stand on the other side of the fence, away from the bleachers. I demanded that that was not enough. This was a second infraction more serious than the first. I wanted the match called. Maybe I was wrong. Maybe I was right. But, we never went back. Grown men calling little boys names is apparently something this tournament is willing to allow. I spoke with her privately and told her in a calm voice that if that’s the kind of families that her tournament wanted to attract, then okay. We would not be attending any more. To this day we have not.”

#

6. **Positively Influence New Players** - Coaches and tournament directors can easily work with newer players to show them the ropes. As a director myself, I don’t often get to talk with everyone, but prior to 8am matches, I assemble everyone at

7:45am and introduce the event and what we are about. We talk about being a tournament dedicated to fair play and sportsmanship. That puts the pressure on me to really deliver the best possible atmosphere for our players. At that time, I remind parents that they are consumers of the tournaments and they vote with their money as to which tournaments are the best. Tournaments are for the players, I tell them, not the other way around.

At the local level, new players come in and out of tournament play. As a parent of a junior, I always took a moment to try to get to know the other parents, and find out a little bit about them. If they wanted some advice, I would give it; if not, just taking a moment to make friendly contact helps make a tournament friendlier and less intimidating. When we encounter people who are new to the competitive side of tennis, we have a rare opportunity to enlighten them to the mission of preserving the dignity of the sport. John O'Sullivan (Changing the Game Project) works very hard to influence parents who are new. Many of these parents are undecided about how they want their kids to play. He wants to influence the newest participants promoting a fun environment, allowing children freedom to play. We all should join John in this task. Slowly, we can eliminate the negatives that are currently driving youth away from sports at an alarming rate. Be a magnet for those undecided parents and players, reach across the net and shake someone's hand.

#

For Players Empowerment

"Integrity is telling myself the truth. And honesty
is telling the truth to other people." -Spencer Johnson

Players, this book is really for you and about you. Perhaps this section is the most important, because you are the only one in direct contact with your opponent. All you really need is the basic desire to have a fair match. If you keep that in mind and do the following, then the winner, whether that's you or your opponent, will have won fair and square.

7. **Have Fun and Play Fair** – A fun match is only possible with fair play and when you are feeling cheated, sports is anything but fun. Ultimately, it is the adults in charge who are responsible for creating an atmosphere of fair play, but as a player you can remind the adults to do so. If the match is not being played fairly, you have permission from the tournament to leave the court in search of a tournament official. If you can't find one quickly, go straight to the tournament desk and ask for a linesperson. Remember, just because you go to get a linesperson does not mean you are calling the opponent a cheater. They need help making calls, and you need help having a fair match. It could be that you are helping them. Maybe they are a cheater but they need to learn. They need to grow and your effort could cause that to happen. On the other hand, if you let them steal the match from you, you are helping no one.

Let me say with all seriousness: Don't let your opponent cheat. They need your help. Remember all the hard work you put into your game? Remember the hours of court time? Remember the sacrifices your parents and coach made to help you improve and play? When you get a linesperson, you are defending that hard work. You are defending the sacrifice of all those who have helped you along the way. But, you are also doing the same for your opponent. And why do that? For the love of the game! Tennis is great sport with a rich heritage. It deserves the respect we give it.

#

8. **Are You Sure?** - Developing a routine is important in tennis. Every player has routines for their serve, between points, between games, and between matches. If you don't have routines, you need to develop some. And while you're at it, I suggest you develop a routine against cheaters. Routines take the emotions out of the equation. Here is the process I teach my players: On the first bad call go to the net and look at the line closely; then, look at your opponent in a respectful way and acknowledge the call. This puts your opponent on notice that you are watching the lines also. If they engage you and ask your opinion, then you know the kind of player you have on your hands and you may have found a new friend. If not, then this simple non-verbal act of looking at them and the line speaks volumes. If there is a second bad call, use the opponent's name: "Mikey, are you sure?" I forbid my students to ask, "Are you sure?" We all know the answer to that question. The simple act of including their name in the question is a powerful personal act that both speaks your friendship towards your opponent and their personal responsibility to you. I urge my players never to ask "Are you sure?" more than once in a match.

Finally, on the third bad call, a linesperson should be called. If the official leaves too quickly, they should be called back at the next infraction. The player should respectfully say to the official, "It is clear to me that my opponent is having trouble calling the lines and we really need your presence for a longer period of time." If a player can learn this simple process and implement it consistently without emotional outburst, they will gain the respect of the tournament officials and the other players.

#

9. **Make friends** who also believe in sportsmanship and include them in your group. At every tournament, have the goal of making one new friend, and see about playing some practice matches with them later if your levels are similar. A large part of the problem of junior tennis cheating at the sectional level is the relative anonymity and lack of community feeling. Create community by finding out about your opponent at the end of the match, win or lose. There have been studies that suggest that when a player feels they are unknown, they worry less about acting poorly. So take a moment to help break through that when you can. Get to know your opponent. You never know, you might make a new friend. Anonymity and alienation empower cheaters, making them feel they can get away with it.

10. **Praise the opponent's good shot** a few times each match without expecting that they will do it for you. Know your opponent's name and use it, "Nice shot, Emily". They may actually return the favor and compliment you. It's harder to make bad calls against someone who is being so nice to you! Be kind to them, and they may be kind in return. Remember, each moment with each player can help make a change in the fairness of your local tournaments.

11. Facebook group **"Players Against Cheating"** (PAC). Start a local chapter of the PAC and create a following that other kids would like to join. Tell some positive stories on the Facebook site.

12. Have the courage to **call your opponent's balls fairly** all the time. Additionally, we all accidentally make a bad call and realize it shortly after, be brave and reverse your call immediately-your opponent will trust you more!

#

Tennis Leadership Action Items

"Leaders become great not because of their power, but because of their ability to empower others." -John Maxwell

13. **Use Your Junior** – Ask your junior players to be court monitors. They'll gain job experience and you'll get great help. They don't need to be empowered to overturn calls. Simply instruct them to be a witness to the match. If they sense that cheating is occurring, they can alert the nearest official, or simply wait for the players to call an official and then they can give their version of events. Most players will feel uncomfortable making a bad call if they know a peer or older junior is there and will see what they have done.

14. Coaches and academies should stress the need for sportsmanship as a way to **protect clientele**. Creating a climate of dishonesty is never good for business. You should teach integrity but you should also let kids who are affected by cheaters know that you are going to do something about the cheating next time it occurs. They need your support. Protect your clientele, not just because they are paying customers but because there are principles involved. No one should be subjected to continued bad behavior. This reflects poorly on your organization and word will get around.

#

15. Governing bodies should **engage with their clientele**. Once per month, a staff member could make 30 phone calls reaching out to players ranked 1, 11, 21... 301, then the next month 2, 12, 22...302, asking: "How are we doing? How would you rate the fair play of tournaments in the last year? We are working to change the culture of junior tournaments for the better." That level of engagement would garner great information and can coax players back into the game. A simple unexpected call to players and parents would create an atmosphere of confidence that the higher-ups care and know what is going on. The amount of good will created by this simple act would be immeasurable.

16. **Officials cannot get trapped** on a single court. There are simply not enough officials to go around. However, I would recommend on the first visit to a court that officials stay for two changeovers. This is long enough to have an impact on the match. If the match swings in the opposite direction during that time, they should consider staying longer. If they leave and are called back to the court, they should stay at least until the end of that set. Why go elsewhere? The squeaky wheel should get the grease.

#

As a final note to tennis leadership, here is a quote from Chad Stoloff of 'The Disciplined Mind': "We only truly control ourselves and how we choose to respond to situations. It is not easy to respond the right way, but the sporting world and the world in general need more role models and less critics. Can we act with principles in mind when the pot is boiling, to model the behavior that we want our children, students, and future leaders of the world to encompass? We need to take responsibility and be the beacon of light leading the way out of the darkness."

#

Parents Cooperating with the Process

Taking Official Action, Giving Measured Responses

"Measure Twice, Cut Once", advice from the Building Trades

17. **Be An Example** – Children learn most of their behavior from their parents. Strive as parents to be paragons of virtue in the area of sportsmanship. Be a light to them and a light to those around you. If we tolerate bad sportsmanship in our children, we allow them to give other players bad experiences. When we do that we run the risk of depleting the player field. Have the expectation that your child will play fair, and hold them to that responsibility.

18. **For the Love of the Game** – Teach them respect for the game and what it means to honor the sport. Without rules and etiquette, sports are no fun. When tournaments become a free-for-all gathering of isolated people, the thrill is gone from the games. I see too many people whose body language suggests: "We are not here to make friends. We are here to beat everyone and come away with a trophy and a higher ranking." This achievement-only pursuit is empty, and makes a tournament environment sterile and lifeless. So let's engage with the people around us and befriend them. Give them a chance to thaw, and maybe they will be less combative. Always appeal to the better side of those around you!

#

19. **Wait for the Best Time**. Parents can take action but they should never insert themselves into a match. This robs both players of one of the virtues that tennis teaches: independence! Parents, when you witness other parents doing this, go to a tournament official and let them know that a parent is influencing the match. This should never be tolerated.

Whatever the situation, whether it's player cheating, meddling parents, or poor officiating, you have the right to inform the powers that be, but try to solve the problem locally first. Unfortunately, it's not always possible for the proper official to be available at all times. People are allowed breaks, can become indisposed or busy with another pressing matter that requires their full attention. It's best to be understanding of the dilemmas faced by tournament officials. Realize that the intervention may not happen in time to be effective. So, if you get no satisfaction, do all the stress exercises you can think of and take notes for the letter you will write to the sanctioning body. Yes, those letters count and are read.

20. **Write a letter.** One frustration among governing bodies is the lack of written complaints. Only written complaints allow for formal follow-up. Keep your letter simple and to the point, keep personalities out of it, focus on the situation, the behavior, the intervention or lack of intervention, the due process and the final result. If you try to make a laundry list of complaints, then you weaken your case. Be brief and specific, and expect follow-up within two weeks or less. You might follow up your letter to find out if

there is a meeting where your letter will be addressed by a committee. Not every problem can be solved immediately, but please do take the time to follow due process.

#

A Final Word to Parents of Difficult Competitors

"Where there is no vision, the people perish."
King Solomon

What if you are the parent of a player who has difficulty in competing fairly? As parents, our best influence will be the discipline of self-control we show at our children's sporting events. Parenting a competitive child who is wired to win at the expense of perfect calls is quite a challenge. Don't allow anyone to demonize your child. But don't allow your child to be a demon on court. I once had a mom of a cheater thank me for giving her boy a code violation for unsportsmanlike conduct. She was ashamed of his behavior. He would get away with the most outlandish calls on a weekly basis and I finally had to put a stop to it.

Working with our sons and daughters is one of the greatest thrills in life. We live and breathe it. Combining love for your family with the love of a sport is one of the supreme joys in life and one of the greatest frustrations. I had my own successes and failures. My son, who was fairly introverted as a youth (cheating isn't always the issue), found it difficult to reach out to his opponents, but we forged ahead and he made great strides. I was quite proud when he started winning sportsmanship awards, and loved it when every year at his high school tennis team banquet, the coach would say, "Here is the kid who really loves tennis". Even now, years later, I run into one of his former opponents, who tell me that Philip was really a good player, and he enjoyed playing against him. Isn't love of the game the most important quality to foster?

21. Set goals for yourself and for your player:

1. Don't allow an opponent to make more than three bad calls against you. Get a linesperson: it will feel good to stand up for yourself.

2. Write one letter of praise to a tournament director, and one letter of constructive criticism to the governing body.

3. Make a new friend of a child and their parent(s) at each event.

4. Use the three goals above or write your own and look for great things to happen in junior tennis.

About the Author

Bill Patton has always been fascinated by strategies in all types of games. With over 25 years experience as a tennis coach, many of which he was able to guide his players into learning better strategy on a white board, on court, and in matches, Bill has a knack for marshaling what a player can do on court out of a position of strength to attack a relative weakness in the opponent. Bill has a B.S in Psychology from California State University, Hayward (now East Bay), and has written his Masters Thesis in Education at National University. He is available to speak in support of this book and the others The Art of Coaching High School Tennis, and Playing Sports Right: Your Way. Both books are available on Bill's website at 720degreecoaching.org. Bill is married and has two youngsters heading off to college.

http://www.bonesoriginalusa.com
Great New Styles in Tennis Clothing
"Be Original, Be Bones!"

http://www.blogtalkradio.com/720degreecoaching
Bill Patton's Radio Blog of Great Coaches and other Resources

GameSmartTennis.com
Match Analysis by Top Notch Coaches
Get YOUR Coach Involved!

Hyper Optimized Practice Learning Utility
HOPLU.com
A great tool to aid in collaboration between players, coaches and parents.

End Cheating in Tennis
http://amzn.to/1SyNVgB

Bill's Tennis Books
http://amzn.to/1K6DTxm

Twitter
@Billpatton720 @hs10scoach @BonesTennisUSA

Email: bill@pattonschooloftennis.com for a free companion resource with this book!

23400753R00061

Printed in Great Britain
by Amazon